Heinemann Educational Publishers
Halley Court, Jordan Hill, Oxford OX2 8EJ
Part of Harcourt Education

Heinemann is the registered trademark of
Harcourt Education Limited

First published 2004

09 08 07 06 05 04
10 9 8 7 6 5 4 3 2 1

British Library Cataloguing in Publication Data is available
from the British Library on request.

ISBN 0 435 32738 0

Typeset by TechType, Abingdon, Oxon

Original illustrations © Harcourt Education Limited, 2003

Printed in the UK by Scotprint
Cover photo: © Rex Features/SIPA

Acknowledgements
Every effort has been made to contact copyright holders of
material reproduced in this book. Any omissions will be
rectified in subsequent printings if notice is given to the
publishers.

Details of written sources
In some sources the wording or sentence structure has been
simplified to ensure that the source is accessible.

p. 7   J.B. Priestley, English Journey (Gollancz, 1934)
p. 61   R. Pearce, Contemporary Britain 1914–79 (Longman,
          1996)
p. 61   ed. R. Broad and S. Fleming, Nella Last's War: A
          Mother's Diary 1938–45 (Sphere, 1983)
p. 61   Doris White, D for Doris, V for Victory (Oakleaf
          Books, 1981)
p. 63   C.R. Schenk, 'Austerity and Boom' in P. Johnson
          ed, Economic, Social and Cultural Change in
          Twentieth Century Britain (Longman, 1994)
p. 73   M. Roberts, Britain 1946–64: The Challenge of
          Change (Oxford University Press, 2001)
p. 73   M. Gilbert, The Roots of Appeasement
          (Weidenfeld & Nicolson, 1966)
p. 73   R. Cockett, Twilight of Truth: Chamberlain,
          Appeasement and the Manipulation of the Press
          (Weidenfeld & Nicolson, 1989)
p. 74   J. Charmley, Chamberlain and the Lost Peace
          (Papermac, 1989)
p. 78   Dilwyn Porter, Never-Never Land: Britain under
          the Conservatives 1951–64 in from Blitz to Blair
          ed. N. Tiratsoo, 1997
p. 121   Eric Hobsbawm, Interesting Times: A Twentieth
          Century Life (Allen Lane, 2002)
p. 121   Norman Tebbit, Upwardly Mobile (Weidenfeld
          & Nicolson, 1988)
p. 121   K.O. Morgan, The People's Peace: British
          History 1945–90 (Oxford University Press,
          1992)
p. 133   P. Hirst (1997), 'Miracle Or Mirage? The
          Thatcher Years 1979–97' in N. Tiratsoo
(ed.), From Blitz to Blair: A New History of Britain since
          1939 (Phoenix, 1998)
p. 133   ed. D. Kavanagh & A. Seldon, The Thatcher
          Effect (Oxford University Press, 1989)
p. 133–134 Norman Tebbit, Upwardly Mobile (Weidenfeld
          & Nicolson, 1988)
p. 148   E. Collins, Killing Rage (Granta, 1998)
p. 150   T.P. Coogan, The Troubles: Ireland's Ordeal
          1966–96 (Arrow, 1996)
p. 150   T. Geraghty, The Irish War: The Military
          History of a Domestic Conflict (HarperCollins,
          2000)
p. 150–151 Brian Faulkner, Memoirs of a Statesman
          (Weidenfeld & Nicolson, 1978)

Photo acknowledgements
The author and publisher would like to thank the following
for permission to reproduce photographs: Corbis/Bettmann
p. 65; Corbis p. 125; Hulton Getty p. 9, p. 11, p. 15, p. 20,
p. 23, p. 35, p. 125; Popperfoto p. 113; Punch p. 27, p. 49;
Topham Picturepoint p. 144; University of Kent Centre for
the Study of Cartoons & Caricature/The Guardian/David
Low p. 53; University of Kent Centre for the Study of
Cartoons & Caricature/Evening Standard/Vicky p. 56;
University of Kent Centre for the Study of Cartoons &
Caricature/The Daily Express/Michael Cummings p. 85;
University of Kent Centre for the Study of Cartoons &
Caricature/The Sunday Telegraph/Nicholas Garland p. 102;
University of Kent Centre for the Study of Cartoons &
Caricature/The Daily Telegraph/Matthew Pritchard p. 120

CONTENTS

HOW TO USE THIS BOOK

This book is divided into two parts. The AS part looks at three distinct periods. Chapters 1 and 2 focus on Britain in the 1930s, explaining the economic and political impact upon Britain of the Great Depression. Chapters 3–5 deal with the Second World War and its effects upon Britain, including Churchill's leadership of the wartime coalition government, the extent of social change, and the reasons behind the startling Labour election victory in 1945. Chapter 6 covers the years from 1945 to 1964, explaining the origins of the Welfare State and the inter-relationship between economic recovery from the war and Britain's attempts to maintain its role as a world power. Summary questions at the end of each chapter will challenge the student to reach analytical explanations and to differentiate between a range of factors.

The A2 part of the book is in three distinct sections, all of which are thematic in approach and which provide a structured framework for dealing with a range of alternative interpretations and perspectives. At A2, students will need to reinforce their knowledge of the detail and their understanding of the issues by wider reading. The first A2 section, on Chamberlain and appeasement, provides an introduction to in-depth historiographical study, drawing on a range of contrasting evidence and interpretation. The second and largest A2 section deals with key themes in British history in the years 1951 to 1997, covering social, economic and European issues as well as political developments. The final A2 section focuses on Britain and Ireland between 1969 and 1998, providing a framework for further in-depth study of the 'Troubles' and for evaluation of the various ways historians and political commentators have viewed the controversial events of the time.

At the end of the AS part and each of the A2 sections, there are assessment exercises. These have been closely modelled on the AS and A2 History specifications. The source-based questions also provide useful material illuminating the topics concerned. Guidance is given as to the skills students should master in approaching the different types of questions.

AS SECTION: POLITICS AND SOCIETY IN BRITAIN, 1929–64

INTRODUCTION: WHAT WAS THE STATE OF BRITAIN IN 1929?

In 1929, Britain was on the eve of the Great Depression. The 1929 Wall Street Crash was one of the most significant turning points of the twentieth century. It is important, however, to remember that History usually looks more clear-cut to later historians than it did to people at the time. There was no instant switch from prosperity to slump in 1929 – there were already significant economic problems before the Crash and the Depression was slow to take effect. It was 1931 before the full extent of the economic crisis became clear.

The year 1929 was also a landmark in British politics. The formation of the second Labour government under **Ramsay MacDonald** (the first had been a short-lived minority government in 1924) represented a significant political development: the point when the Labour Party replaced the Liberals as the main opponent of the Conservatives in Britain's two-party system. Many on the Left hoped (and many on the Right feared) that the way was open for the rise and rise of socialism. They were probably right on general principle but the process turned out to be much slower and more complex than expected, partly but not only, because Ramsay MacDonald's 1929 Labour government unluckily came to power just in time to inherit the economic earthquake of the Great Depression.

Both in politics and in economics, the situation of 1929 reflected the huge impact upon Britain, and upon Europe as a whole, of the First World War. The Great War had unleashed a cycle of revolutionary changes, from votes for women in Britain to the rise of communism and the Soviet Union; from the emergence of the USA as a world power to the rise of fascism. The war and the post-war peace settlement had also dealt a heavy blow to colonial empires: one of the continuing problems for Britain in the interwar years was the issue of the Empire (especially India) and how to deal with independence movements. Thus, in many ways, Britain was still struggling in 1929 to come to terms with the aftershocks of the Second World War.

To explain what happened to Britain between 1929 and 1951, History students need to answer the following questions:

- What was the situation at the beginning?
- What was the situation at the end?
- In between, what changed?
- What stayed the same?

The following snapshot summary of Britain in 1929 is necessarily brief and oversimplified; however, it provides a starting point from which the History of Britain after 1929 can be judged.

Economics

The British economy was facing a painful period of adjustment in the 1920s. Several historians (see Key texts), have argued that Britain's economic position had been in long-term decline since well before 1914, noting, for example, that Germany had overtaken Britain's role as the leading economic power in Europe by about 1890. The First World War then added to Britain's difficulties by dislocating traditional markets and by building up huge government debts. Among the economic worries of the late 1920s, the following loomed large.

- **High unemployment.** The annual average rate of unemployment was never less than 1 million during the 1920s. The General Strike of 1926 was caused by pressure to reduce miners wages and was a sign of the structural problems in the economy.
- **The decline of staple industries.** Key British industries, above all shipbuilding, coal mining and textiles, were struggling with changed markets and increased foreign competition. Britain's railway companies had not paid any dividends to shareholders since 1923.

KEY TEXTS

A. Gamble *Britain's Decline* Macmillan (1985)

C. Barnett *The Lost Victory* (1995)

R. Pope Britain's *Economic performance since 1914* (1998)

- **The Gold Standard.** After the First World War, the **international financial system** was very unstable. Britain returned to the Gold Standard in 1925 (a decision taken by **Winston Churchill**, then Chancellor in Baldwin's Conservative government) hoping that it would lead to financial stability and help economic modernisation. In fact, the Gold Standard probably increased the rigidity of the economy. One key moment in the crisis of 1931 was the decision of a Labour Chancellor to take Britain off the Gold Standard and to devalue the pound against the US dollar.

Politics

By the late 1920s, all three main political parties faced the prospect of fundamental changes.

- The Liberal Party had already begun the terminal decline that ended with virtual wipe-out in the 1951 election. The high profile of the great Liberal leader, **David Lloyd George**, tended to hide the full extent of Liberal decline; however, the anti-Conservative vote was shifting irreversibly towards Labour.
- The Labour Party was correspondingly on the rise. Labour enthusiasts were convinced that the 'Age of Socialism' had arrived. The first Labour government, in 1924, was short-lived but it was felt that the formation of Ramsay MacDonald's second Labour government in 1929 was a true beginning. At that time, also, there was little or no awareness of the realities of the Soviet Union or the evils to come under **Joseph Stalin**. It was possible for Labour enthusiasts to be starry-eyed about Soviet communism.
- The Conservatives were still the 'natural party of government', backed by the strengths of the so-called 'establishment'. **Stanley Baldwin**'s reassuring, pipe-smoking image as prime minister from 1924–9 typified the appeal of the Conservatives as the safe choice. The Conservatives were backed by the vast majority of national newspapers, by business, by the middle classes and significant parts of the working class. Nevertheless, the Conservatives were quite frightened by the rise of Labour and by the power of the trade unions. The General Strike of 1926 had been a nasty shock. Many Conservatives felt that the party needed to modernise.

Sights and sounds

Historians must always try to achieve the almost impossible task of understanding the context in which people lived. The Britain of 1929 was very different from the Britain of the late 1990s in countless ways.

- It looked different. Mostly, it looked black: buildings, such as the great Liverpool waterfront, were soot-black; men's clothing was generally black or grey; the air was black from millions of coal fires and industrial pollution. There were no motorways or multi-storey car parks; residential streets were mostly car-free and children played outside their houses. Town centres were crowded and busy, dominated by department stores and double-decker trams.
- It sounded different. Radios were relatively few, and never outdoors, and television was unknown. The cinema sounded different: 1929 was the year that mass audiences got used to talking pictures rather than silent films. Everywhere there were the noises of steam trains, factories and street sellers.
- It smelt different. Modern affluence has spread shampoos and deodorants through almost all levels of society; the smells of 1929 Britain included more body odour, along with vast clouds of cigarette smoke in public places and the now long-forgotten smell of horse manure in those streets served by delivery vans.
- It was less mobile. Working-class people were relatively enclosed in their own neighbourhoods. Holidays abroad were for the elite; the masses went to seaside resorts, such as Southend, Scarborough and Southport. Millions travelled to work on foot or by bicycle.
- It *felt* different. The church played a significant role in people's lives, both in leisure and social activities. School and family life was more formal; there was no such thing as youth culture.

The list of differences could continue, yet it is important to take a balanced view: there is always continuity as well as change. In the Britain of 1929, people had most of the same concerns as their grandchildren's generation 70 years on. Football fans were obsessed; relationships were a priority; advertising was as sharp and ever-present as it is today, different only in style and outward appearance.

Above all, the British people at the end of the 1920s did not feel themselves to be living quaint and old-fashioned lives, as might seem to be the case from black-and-white photographs. They knew that they lived in very modern times full of new ideas, new inventions and up-to-the-minute fashion magazines. Historians must always realise that what happened in the past was not old-fashioned when it happened.

KEY THEMES OF THE AS SECTION

In assessing the important trends and developments between 1929 and 1951, some key themes can be identified:

- the economic impact of the Depression and its effects on society
- the problems facing the Labour Party from 1931 and why it remained in the political wilderness until 1945
- the threat of political extremism, from both Left and Right
- the dominance of the National Government in the 1930s and how it dealt with the economic and political problems of the time
- Britain's reaction to the threat of war and the policy of appeasement; then the 'Phoney War'; finally, Total War
- how the Second World War was fought and to what extent the war changed British society
- why the Labour Party won a landslide victory in 1945 and how successfully it dealt with economic crisis and recovery in the years to 1951
- to what extent Britain's foreign and imperial position was maintained in the post-war world.

This book will not provide complete answers to all these questions; however, it will help AS students to make a start.

CHAPTER 1

What was the economic and social impact of the Great Depression?

INTRODUCTION

The Wall Street Crash occurred in October 1929. This collapse of the stock market in the USA was the trigger for a deep and lasting economic slump in the world economy. This slump was not sudden and did not hit all countries equally, or at the same time. Between 1930 and 1933, the

Towns and cities in 1930s Britain (Towns and cities underlined were in areas of economic hardship.)

KEY THEME

The impact of the depression on Britain

Historians express conflicting opinions about the impact of the 1930s Depression. This is because the social and economic impact upon Britain was extremely uneven. In parts of the country, the slump could hardly have been worse, with massive unemployment, extreme poverty and long-term hopelessness. Towns such as Wigan and Jarrow became famous as symbols of deprivation. Elsewhere, however, the 1930s was a time of affluence, with new industries, rising living standards and increased leisure opportunities (see the map Towns in the 1930s).

Depression steadily worsened, marked by a growing banking crisis, the collapse of exports and, above all, by mass unemployment. The British economy was badly affected by the Great Depression. There were already structural economic problems in the 1920s, with relatively high unemployment and stagnation in traditional staple industries such as shipbuilding and textiles. The world depression intensified these long-term trends; the 'Hungry Thirties' had begun.

Regional differences

These regional differences represent not so much conflicting opinions as conflicting truths; it is a matter of fact, not opinion, that some areas endured misery while other parts of Britain lived in much more comfortable circumstances. What historians have disagreed about is the overall performance of the British economy in the 1930s – whether it was overall a time of economic failure and decline, except for a few pockets of affluence, or a time of economic success, except for some areas of special hardship.

In 1934, the author J.B. Priestley described in his acclaimed book, *English Journey*, the differences within society in 1930s Britain. This description has been quoted repeatedly but, despite its familiarity, has never been bettered and deserves to be repeated again here:

> *In my travels, I had seen a lot of England. There was, first, Old England, the country of cathedrals and manor houses and inns; guidebook and quaint highways-and-byways England. Then, second, there was the nineteenth-century England, the industrial England of coal, iron, steel, cotton, wool, railways; of thousands of rows of little houses all alike, of town halls, mills, warehouses, railway stations, slag-heaps, fried-fish shops, pubs. This England makes up the larger part of the Midlands and the North but it is not being added to and has no new life being poured into it. The third England was the new post-war England. America, I suppose, was its birthplace. This is the England of arterial roads, of filling stations, of giant cinemas and dance halls and cafes, of bungalows with tiny garages, of cocktail bars, Woolworths, motor-coaches, wireless, hiking, swimming pools and factory girls looking like actresses.*

J.B. Priestley, *English Journey* (Gollancz, 1934)

The gulf between the old industrial England and the new suburban England has sometimes been characterised as the 'North-South Divide', but this is too simplistic. There were plenty of examples of the depressed 'North' in south-east England; and many pockets of the affluent 'South' in parts of the North and the Midlands. In the following pages, evidence is assembled to support the contrasting impressions of Britain in the 1930s: first the pessimistic view of the Thirties as a time of hardship and dangerous social divisions; then the optimistic view of the Thirties as a decade of suburban affluence.

THE CASE FOR THE 'HUNGRY THIRTIES'

- **The collapse of staple industries.** Many industries that were already in decline before 1929 were forced into recession, with massive cutbacks and closures. Such industries tended to be specialised in **plant** and machinery, and in the skills of the workforce. New industries developed elsewhere, leaving behind massive dereliction.
- **Mass unemployment.** Unemployment doubled between 1929 and 1931, from 1.4 million to 2.9 million (see the table below). By 1932, 35 per cent of coalminers, 48 per cent of steelworkers and 62 per cent of workers in shipbuilding were unemployed.
- **Demoralisation.** Dependence on the dole and the **Means Test** was widely seen as humiliating, taking away the dignity of working men. These difficulties placed many marriages under strain, and there were

UNEMPLOYMENT IN BRITAIN IN THE 1930S

Year	Total Workforce (000s)	Total Unemployment (000s)	Unemployment Rate (Percentage)
1928	17123	1278	10.8
1930	17016	1979	16.1
1932	16644	2828	22.1
1934	17550	2170	16.7
1936	17890	1749	13.1
1938	19243	1800	12.9

instances of men fighting with each other for work. Those workers worst affected by unemployment were the least mobile – the people for whom it was hardest to uproot and move long distances to find new work.

- **Child poverty and malnutrition.** In 1936, the social researcher Seebohm Rowntree estimated that 52 per cent of very young children were living below the **poverty line**. Other experts estimated that 20 million people were underfed.

- **Social divisions.** Many towns and districts felt cut off and forgotten during the Depression. In 1936, the left wing Labour MP Ellen Wilkinson led a protest march from the north-east town of Jarrow to publicise the desperate economic conditions in the 'town that was murdered'. The Jarrow March made the town famous; however, Jarrow was typical of many depressed areas.

- **The rise of extremism.** There was a significant rise in support for the both the extreme Left and the extreme Right. This led to outbreaks of political violence, notably in 1934 and 1936 (see page 23).

THE CASE FOR THE 'DAWN OF AFFLUENCE'

- **The rise of new industries.** Although the old export-based staple industries suffered badly in the 1930s, there was a compensating growth of newer enterprises. These new industries were generally concentrated in London, the South East and the West Midlands. They were powered by electricity rather than coal and moved their goods by road rather than rail; this emphasised the move away from the traditional coalfields. Britain became the second biggest car producer in the world. Electrical engineering was another growth industry.

- **A housing boom.** More houses were built in Britain in the 1930s than in any decade before. The house-building boom also boosted the construction industry and the market in consumer goods.

- **Rising living standards.** Car ownership reached 3 million by 1939. Consumer goods such as radios, cookers, vacuum cleaners and fashionable clothes were widely available and much cheaper than before.

- **Improvements in real wages.** During the Depression, the fall in prices was bigger than any fall in wages. **Real wages** rose steadily through the decade and were

KEY TERMS

Poverty line This was a calculation by economists to assess the level of family income below which it was not possible to maintain adequate nutrition and health.

Jarrow marchers 1936.

KEY TERM

Real wages Wages defined in terms of how much can be purchased with them.

WAGES, PRICES & REAL EARNINGS 1930–1938			
Year	Wage Rates	Retail Prices	Real Wages
1930	(100.00)	(100.00)	(100.00)
1932	96.3	91.1	105.7
1934	96.4	89.2	108.1
1936	100.2	93.0	107.7
1938	106.3	98.7	107.7

significantly higher than in the 1920s. Put simply, those people who *had* jobs in the 1930s were better off than before (see the table of wages and earnings above).

- **The growth of the retail industry.** High streets all over Britain had new chain stores, such as Marks and Spencer, Boots and Woolworths.
- **Increased leisure opportunities.** The 1930s was the great age of cinema, following the birth of talking pictures in the late 1920s. Radio was a source of cheap entertainment and widened horizons. Cars and coaches made weekend excursions easily available: the 1930s was the first decade of holiday traffic jams.
- **Effective action by the National Government.** The National Government was continuously in power, with a large majority, from 1931–1945. It was able to take a number of measures that had some limited success in alleviating the worst effects of the Depression. These measures included maintaining **low interest rates**, the **Unemployment Act of 1934**, and the **Special Areas Act** of 1935. The economy also benefited from the decision to take Britain off the Gold Standard in September 1931, which devalued the pound against the US dollar and thus helped exports to recover lost markets (see Chapter 2, pages 19–20).

The impact of the 1930s Depression, varied markedly across Britain. For those in work and those who were flexible enough to move, it was possible to achieve a life of suburban comfort. For those trapped in the areas of the declining traditional industries, hardship was very difficult to escape from (see the map and table of unemployment figures on pages 6 and 8).

KEY FACTS

Low interest rates charged by banks meant that 'cheap money' could be borrowed for mortgages and hire purchase.

KEY ACTS

Unemployment Act, 1934
This Act set up the National Unemployment Assistance Board, aimed at helping unemployed workers retrain and move to areas of employment.

Special Areas Act, 1935
This Act provided £2 million in aid to depressed areas in Wales, Scotland and the North East (this was extended by the Special Areas Amendment Act in 1937).

A photograph
showing prosperity
in Britain in the
1930s.

KEY THEME

The image of the Hungry Thirties was powerful, emotive and long-lasting. Books like Walter Greenwood's *Love on the Dole* (1933) and George Orwell's *Road to Wigan Pier* (1937) became enduring classics and moulded attitudes over many years.

KEY TEXT

D. Aldcroft *The Interwar economy 1918–39* (1970)

The impact of the Depression also varied according to time. The slump was at its worst from 1931, when unemployment was between 2.5 million and 3 million. From 1934 onwards, there was a considerable degree of recovery: unemployment fell to 2.2 million in 1934, 2 million in 1935. and to 1.5 million by 1937, a level similar to that before the Crash. In 1938, the danger of Britain slipping back into recession was avoided because rapid rearmament provided a stimulus to the economy, especially in the steel and engineering industries. The degree of economic recovery should not be overstated; for it was not until the 1940s and the Second World War that Britain moved to economic growth and full employment. Nevertheless, there was relative recovery from 1934.

CONCLUSION

The social and economic impact of the Depression in Britain in the 1930s was mixed, varying sharply according to time and place. Most modern historians tend to agree with Derek Aldcroft that the 1930s was a time of relative economic success, and certainly not notably worse than the 1920s. The impact of the world depression after 1929 was less severe in Britain than in other countries.

When the Second World War ended after years of a national collective war effort, the 1945 general election was fought largely on the issues of the bitter memories of the

1930s. Labour's electoral slogan in 1945 was 'Never Again'; key to Labour's landslide victory was the promise to introduce a **Welfare State** and thus ensure that the hardships and divisions of the Thirties were not repeated.

At the time, however, attitudes were very different. There was no chance of a Labour landslide in the 1930s. Whatever the economic and social impact of the Depression may have been, its *political* impact brought down the Macdonald government in 1929 and condemned the Labour Party to long years of electoral failure and internal divisions.

SUMMARY QUESTIONS

1. How and why did the impact of the Great Depression affect different parts of British society in such different ways?

2. How effectively did the National Government deal with the social and economic problems caused by the depression?

CHAPTER 2

How was British politics affected by the Great Depression?

WHY DID THE SECOND LABOUR GOVERNMENT COLLAPSE IN 1931?

The 1929 general election seemed to mark the breakthrough of the Labour Party into national politics. In 1924, Labour had been briefly in power as a weak minority government. In 1929, a number of factors placed Labour in a much stronger position.

- Labour won 287 seats, compared with 191 in 1924.
- Labour was still dependent on Liberal support but was now clearly the dominant party – the Liberals had declined from 155 seats to 59.
- Ramsay MacDonald was a high-profile leader and ex-prime minister, able to benefit from his experience in 1924.
- The failure of the General Strike in 1926 meant that MacDonald's moderate approach had been vindicated, as opposed to the more radical policies proposed on the left wing of the party.

However, the high hopes of 1929 quickly led to failure and disillusionment. The new Labour government lasted just over two years before collapsing in a storm of bitter divisions and recriminations. After 1931, Labour remained in the political wilderness for the rest of the 1930s and returned to power in 1945 only because of the upheavals of the Second World War. Ever since 1931, Ramsay MacDonald and the second Labour government had become symbols of failure and betrayal.

REASONS FOR ELECTORAL DEFEAT

The impact of the Great Depression

Some of the reasons for the disasters that hit Labour in 1931 are obvious. The second Labour government came to power at the wrong moment, just in time for the economic consequences of the Wall Street Crash and the gathering world depression. It is worth noting that all over the western world, those governments that were in power in 1929 were each voted out by 1932: in Germany, for example, the promising **SPD coalition** of 1928 broke apart in 1930; in the USA, the Depression forced out President Hoover; in France, there were three changes of government between 1930 and 1933.

There are, however, many other factors to explain the failure of the Labour government in 1931 and, perhaps even more importantly, why the Labour Party was so badly damaged by what happened in 1931. These include:

- the in-built power of the anti-socialist 'establishment', including the business and the so-called '**Tory Press**'
- the cautious, orthodox economic policies followed by MacDonald's Chancellor, **Philip Snowden** – the Labour government rejected more **radical and expansionary policies** recommended by **Oswald Mosley** and others
- the lack of political realism on the left wing of the Labour Party for example, refusing to accept the need for spending cuts
- above all, the controversial role of Ramsay MacDonald himself.

Labour's economic policy

When Ramsay MacDonald returned to power in 1929, he hoped above all to achieve two things: to reduce unemployment and to prove that Labour could be a responsible government, able to keep the nation's finances safe. Almost from the first, however, unemployment rose steeply and carried on rising. By 1931, there was also a growing financial crisis. MacDonald had little expertise in economic policy, being more at home in foreign affairs. He, together with his Chancellor, Philip Snowden, was also naturally cautious. The government set up an Economic Advisory Council in 1930 but spent most of its time following 'safe', financially orthodox policies.

Some individuals campaigned for more government intervention and for public works schemes. Such voices included the economist J.M. Keynes, the Liberal leader Lloyd George and, from within the Labour Party, Oswald Mosley. Rejection of his economic proposals prompted Mosley to leave the Labour Party in 1930 and to start his

KEY FACT

SPD coalition The moderate socialist-led government in Weimar Germany, which split and collapsed in 1930 over the issue of cuts in public spending.

KEY TERM

'**Tory Press**' The Labour party and its supporters regarded national newspapers in Britain as being permanently pro-Conservative and anti-Labour.

KEY PERSON

Philip Snowden (1864-1937) A leading Labour politician, who was Chancellor of the Exchequer in the governments of 1924 and 1929. In the great split of 1931 Snowden stayed loyal to Ramsay MacDonald, but later turned against him.

KEY FACT

Radical expansionary policies Oswald Mosley supported the idea of using state spending to create jobs – his economic ideas were somewhat similar to those of Mussolini's Italy. In 1930, Mosley put forward a memorandum to the Labour cabinet in 1930; when it was rejected he broke away to form his own party.

KEY PERSON

Oswald Mosley (1896-1980) Mosley was born into a wealthy family. Wounded in the Great War, he became a Conservative MP in 1918 and then a Labour MP in 1926. After he split with MacDonald's cabinet in 1930, he formed a new party in 1931. In 1932 he set up the BUF (British Union of Fascists).

breakaway New Party, leading eventually to the formation of the British Union of Fascists (see pages 22–23). MacDonald and Snowden continued to be reluctant to experiment.

The May Report, 1931

In 1931, the MacDonald government appointed the May Committee, headed by a leading financier, to make a report and recommendations. The key proposals of the May Committee were widespread pay cuts across the public sector and, most controversially, a cut of 20 per cent in unemployment benefit. These proposals caused a storm of protest within the Cabinet and the Labour movement, especially, the trade unions. It was this controversy over the May Committee that eventually brought MacDonald down.

MacDonald and Snowden continued to insist that the cuts were the only way forward; a majority of the Cabinet continued to oppose them. MacDonald went to see King George V to resign but was persuaded to stay on as prime minister at the head of a **National Government**, which included four Conservatives, four Labour ministers and two Liberals.

This move split the Labour Party badly. Only a handful of Labour MPs followed Ramsay MacDonald into the National Government, with the bulk of the Party in angry opposition. The Liberal Party was similarly split and never really recovered. In September 1931, Philip Snowden produced a special budget, raising income tax, cutting public sector pay and cutting unemployment benefit by ten per cent (not the 20 per cent recommended by the May Committee). Then, in October, MacDonald called a general election in which the National Government fought against Labour and Liberal opponents Labour inevitably did badly, gaining only 52 seats, compared with 287 in 1929.

The fall of Ramsay MacDonald

The developments between the publication of the May Report in July 1931 and the election disaster in October caused Ramsay MacDonald to be widely denounced as a traitor to his own party. The attacks on MacDonald were bitter, founded on a number of charges against him:

- that he had not followed socialist economic policies but allowed himself to be influenced by orthodox capitalist

Ramsay MacDonald.

thinking; for example, by giving too much influence to the anti-socialist financiers who made up the May Committee

- that he had betrayed the working classes by pushing through cuts in unemployment benefit, thus hitting those people experiencing the most hardship
- that he had specifically promised *not* to call a general election and had almost immediately broken his pledge; to make matters worse, he had not resigned but had fought the election on the same side as the Conservatives and against his own party by working with the National Government
- that he had willingly collaborated with the Conservatives and that they, not the Labour party, had gained most from the deal
- that he had become vain and snobbish and had lost touch with his working-class roots and his own party; he was accused of 'selling out' to his new upper-crust colleagues
- that by continuing as prime minister until 1935 he had provided a convenient image of national unity for what was in reality a Conservative-dominated government.

Ramsay MacDonald's career and reputation never recovered from 1931. He resigned as prime minister in 1935 and died soon afterwards, regarded always as the man who split the party. Even the mild-mannered **Clement Attlee** described MacDonald's actions in 1931 as 'the greatest political betrayal in the history of this country'.

Despite all this, many politicians and historians have defended MacDonald, for the following reasons.

- At the time, the king and most of the national press applauded MacDonald for putting the country ahead of his party; **Neville Chamberlain** thought MacDonald had sacrificed his career from a sense of national duty.
- MacDonald had not planned to stay in power when the Labour government came to an end; he was persuaded to stay on against his will.
- The extent of the economic crisis in 1931 was so severe that drastic measures were required; MacDonald was realistic about this – his party was not. He thus became a scapegoat for Labour's fall from power when it was certain to happen anyway.

KEY PEOPLE

Clement Attlee (1863-1967) Attlee served in the Great War and became a Labour MP and private secretary to Ramsay MacDonald. In 1935 he succeeded George Lansbury as leader of the Labour party. He was deputy prime minister in Churchill's wartime coalition and then prime minister from 1945 to 1951.

Neville Chamberlain (1869-1940) son of the famous Conservative politician Joseph Chamberlain and Lord Mayor of Birmingham. He became a Conservative MP in 1918 and was Chancellor of the Exchequer from 1931 to 1937, when he succeeded Baldwin as prime minister.

KEY TEXT

D. Marquand *Ramsay Macdonald* Cape (1977)

WHAT WERE THE EFFECTS OF 1931 ON THE LABOUR PARTY?

Ramsay MacDonald's 'betrayal' was not simply his decision to split the Party and head the National Government; it was also his decision to call a general election in October 1931 (despite firm promises at the time that he would not). As Labour loyalists feared, this election came at a disastrous time for the Party. Labour was left with only 52 seats; the National Government had 554 seats. The results of the local municipal elections were almost as bad. The Labour Party was badly divided and demoralised and was to remain in the political wilderness for the rest of the 1930s. At the 1935 general election, Labour made a recovery but the National Government retained a massive majority.

Conservative strengths

It seemed as if there was an in-built Conservative dominance of British politics that would always keep Labour out of power. These Conservative strengths included:

- the image of Stanley Baldwin and the National Government
- pro-Conservative attitudes in the national press and among business leaders
- the so-called 'Conservative establishment' associated with the monarchy, the legal profession, the elite universities and public schools
- the idea of the Conservatives as the 'party of economic competence'.

Labour weaknesses

Many people, even Labour supporters, doubted if Labour would ever form a government again. The Party was perceived to have political handicaps it would never overcome. These included:

KEY FACT

Experienced Labour politicians Able politicians, such as Arthur Henderson and George Lansbury, were victims of Labour's weakness in the early 1930s.

- the memory of 1931 and internal party divisions symbolised by deep bitterness towards Ramsay MacDonald
- the disappearance of a generation of **experienced Labour politicians** who lost their seats in 1931; the little-known and unexciting Clement Attlee became Party leader in 1935

- the idea that Labour governments were associated with economic disasters and would never be trusted by business
- the feeling that Labour's ideology was too left-wing, foreign and unpatriotic.

Labour's divisions appeared deep and MacDonald remained a hate-figure long after his death. However, in reality, the Party had been less badly damaged than appeared. Electoral support for Labour held up remarkably well in the Labour heartlands and, even in 1931, the total Labour vote was above 30 per cent. Indeed, the Labour Party did not suffer a major collapse in the 1930s and extremist political groupings failed to make a breakthrough: neither the Mosleyites on the Right nor the Communists on the Left were able to win mass support from traditional Labour voters. In the 1935 general election, Labour recovered to a position not that different from that of 1929.

Political recovery in the 1930s

There were, in fact, a number of factors leading to some sort of Labour recovery in the 1930s. Though often underrated, Clement Attlee proved to be a quietly capable leader. Throughout the 1930s, Labour did well in by-elections. Some political commentators have suggested that any general election at the end of the 1930s would have seen further increases in the Labour vote (there wasn't one because the war began in 1939). Although the Labour Party would probably not have been able to win, it certainly would have done better than in 1935.

Labour's defeats in the 1930s were made to look worse than they actually were by the special peculiarities of Britain's **'first-past-the-post' electoral system**. In 1935, a relatively small increase in the Labour vote, from 31 per cent to 36 per cent, resulted in three times as many Labour MPs than in 1931. For the same reason, the 1945 'landslide' looked much more dramatic than the actual number of votes moving towards Labour. In 1951, when Labour lost power again, the total Labour vote was only slightly down on the 1945 figure.

Year	Percentage Voting	Number of seats
1929	33	287
1931	31	52
1935	36	154
1945	40	393
1950	38	264
1951	39	259

The Labour Vote: percentage of votes and number of seats won in general elections, 1929–51.

KEY FACT

'First-past-the-post' electoral system British MPs can be elected with any majority, from one to 25 000 or more. This means that a relatively small swing in total votes can cause huge changes in the number of seats that are won and lost.

KEY DEBATE

Was the National Government a source of stability and reassurance, enabling Britain to survive the 1930s without the disasters that overtook other countries in continental Europe? Or was the National Government complacent and inactive, failing to take the measures that might have saved Britain's depressed industrial regions from the hardships of mass unemployment? Did Britain recover from the world depression *because* of the National Government or in spite of it?

KEY TERM

Appeasement is the policy of negotiating and making concessions in order to avoid the danger of war.

KEY PERSON

Adolf Hitler (1889-1945) an Austrian corporal who founded the Nazi Party in 1920, he became Chancellor of Germany in 1933, and then established himself as dictator. In the 1930s, many people in Britain regarded him as a dangerous extremist; others saw him as a potential ally against Communism.

THE NATIONAL GOVERNMENT,1931–40

The National Government was dominated throughout the 1930s by the Conservatives. Labour suffered for years from the trauma of 1931 and the Liberals were also badly split and in decline. Although Ramsay MacDonald lingered on as prime minister until 1935, the key personalities of the National Government were Stanley Baldwin, who became prime minister in 1935 and Neville Chamberlain, who was Chancellor from 1931 until he succeeded Baldwin as prime minister in 1937.

It was the National Government, therefore, that had to steer Britain through the difficulties of the Great Depression: there is considerable disagreement about how well they did.

The nation's choice

The National Government was certainly in tune with opinion in the country. It not only won a convincing victory in the crisis election of 1931, it won another massive victory in 1935. If there had been a general election in 1939 or 1940, all commentators agree that the National Government would have won again, though perhaps with a reduced majority. There was never any uncertainty in the 1930s about who would be in power.

The fact that the government was a coalition of elements of all the major parties meant that it faced no serious opposition from mainstream politics. Many working-class voters supported it; in 1935, the National Government won all the seats in several industrial towns such as Blackburn and Sunderland. The National Government was broadly accepted in the 1930s – it was one of very few governments in British history that was supported by more than 50 per cent of the electorate. Even **appeasement** was popular at the time; it was only after the outbreak of the Second World War that it became the norm to attack the National Government for allowing **Hitler** off the leash and for being uncaring about the 'Hungry Thirties'.

Economic policies

The economic policies of the National Government were mostly cautious and traditionally Conservative however, there were a number of attempts to use state intervention to soften the impact of the Depression. The key policies included:

- cuts in unemployment benefit (that MacDonald's Labour Cabinet had failed to agree to after the May Committee report); these cuts lasted until 1934
- the decision to come off the Gold Standard in 1931. This was policy that Labour had avoided for fear of upsetting the 'establishment'. The result was that the value of the pound fell by about 30 per cent. As a result, the government was able to reduce interest rates to two per cent, which had a beneficial effect on the economy
- the Import Duties Act of 1932, which brought in a protective tariff of ten per cent on goods from outside the empire
- the Special Areas Act of 1935, which provided £2 million in aid to depressed areas in Wales, Scotland and the North East (this was extended by the Special Areas Amendment Act in 1937)
- the Unemployment Act of 1934, which set up the National Unemployment Assistance Board, aimed at helping unemployed workers retrain and move to areas of employment
- various measures to rationalise and reorganise struggling industries: the Iron and Steel Federation in 1934, the Shipping Act of 1935, and the Cotton Industry Reorganisation Act of 1936.

These actions were mostly cautious and with a small-scale impact; they did not lead to any significant economic recovery, though they may have helped to soften some of the worst effects of the Depression. Overall, Britain experienced a slow, patchy economic recovery from 1934.

The leadership of Stanley Baldwin

Baldwin was a dominating figure in the 1930s, even though he was prime minister for only two years, from 1935–37. He was a familiar and reassuring personality, who had twice been prime minister in the 1920s; he was seen as a man of moderation and common sense. He was not only popular with the middle classes but also with many working-class voters, especially women. Baldwin was also a very effective Party leader; it was extremely difficult

Stanley Baldwin.

for any right-wing elements to challenge the government while he was in office. Even Winston Churchill, who frequently clashed with Baldwin on India and appeasement, had little impact on Conservative politics before 1940.

The Abdication Crisis of 1936. One of Baldwin's great successes was his smooth handling of the Abdication Crisis in 1936. It appeared as if the constitutional storm caused by King Edward VIII's decision to marry the twice-divorced US socialite Wallis Simpson might bring down the monarchy itself and inflict lasting damage to the political system and Church of England. Many in the Conservative Party, including Churchill, wished to support the king. Baldwin took a more calm and realistic view. In the event, Edward VIII chose to abdicate in favour of his brother, George VI. The expected constitutional crisis never really happened, something for which many observers gave Baldwin most of the credit. When Baldwin handed over to Neville Chamberlain in 1937, the position of the National Government was as secure as ever.

WHY DID POLITICAL EXTREMISM WIN LITTLE NATIONAL SUPPORT?

In continental Europe, the 1930s was the decade of political extremes, of the struggle between communism and fascism. In Britain, this was not the case. There was a period when Oswald Mosley and his Blackshirts of the British Union of Fascists (BUF) gained national prominence. There was also a rise in the activities of, and support for, the Communist Party of Great Britain (CPGB). In some industrial cities such as Leeds, and in London's East End, there were frequent outbreaks of political violence. However, political extremism never made a breakthrough; it remained on the fringes of British politics.

Communism

Since the Depression seemed to mark the collapse of the capitalist system, it is not surprising that the 1930s saw a rise in support for the communists. Many on the Left felt that the failures of the Labour government indicated that more radical socialist policies were needed. The rise of Hitler in Germany, **Mussolini** in Italy and later of **General Franco** in Spain, not to mention Mosley in Britain,

KEY PEOPLE

Benito Mussolini (1883-1945) the founder of Italian Fascism in 1919 and Leader (Il Duce) of Italy from 1922 until he was overthrown in 1943. In the 1920s and 1930s many in the West admired Mussolini for his supposedly successful economic policies.

General Franco (1892-1975) Franco led the right-wing military revolt against the Spanish Republic in 1936. Helped by Mussolini and Hitler, Franco's forces achieved victory in the Spanish Civil War by 1939. Franco remained dictator of Spain until his death in 1975.

convinced many that only the communists would stand firm against the fascist threat.

The communists, therefore, made gains in the 1930s. The Communist Party of Great Britain (CPGB) increased its membership from 2500 to 18,000; the Party newspaper, *The Daily Worker,* saw a big rise in circulation. Communists also became prominent in several trade unions, such as the electricians and the dockers. The CPGB had set up the National Unemployed Workers' Movement in 1921 and this organisation gained support in the 1930s by providing help and advice for the unemployed. Working-class communists fought numerous street battles against the British Union of Fascists, most famously in the 'Battle of Cable Street' in London in 1936. The **Left Book Club** was started in 1936. There was a lot of support for the Republican cause in the **Spanish Civil War**. A number of Cambridge intellectuals such as **Burgess, Maclean and Philby** began spying for the Soviet Union.

However, these developments did not signal a breakthrough for communism in Britain. To succeed, the communists would have had either to replace the Labour Party as the chief party of the Left or join with Labour in a socialist alliance. The Labour Party refused either to collapse or to accept communist affiliation; most left-wingers continued to fight their cause within the Labour Party rather than break away from it. In addition, the communists never had a well-known personality as leader who could attract national support.

Mosley and the BUF

Where the Communist Party had no dominant personality, the British Union of Fascists did. Oswald Mosley was a powerful speaker with a glamorous image. He was a rich man and a talented politician. One journalist claimed that Mosley was 'the only man who could have been leader of either the Labour Party or of the Conservatives'. For a time, Mosley seemed as if he might make the BUF a serious force in British politics.

Mosley was a member of the 1929 Labour government. He might well have stayed there; however, he became impatient when the Labour Cabinet rejected his **Memorandum** in 1930. He left and formed his own New

Oswald Mosley and his Blackshirts at the rally of British Union of Fascists in 1930s

Party but won no seats in the 1931 general election. In 1932, Mosley formed another party, strongly influenced by the example of Mussolini in Italy – the British Union of Fascists. The BUF gained support from ex-soldiers, the unemployed and working-class youths with a taste for violence. The BUF was also strongly anti-Semitic. By 1934, membership had risen to 50,000. Lord Rothermere, the owner of the *Daily Mail,* provided valuable financial support and favourable publicity.

After reaching this peak, membership of the BUF fell back sharply. This was partly because Mosley made mistakes. He was a charismatic leader but weak in organisation and tactics. He alienated many within his own inner circle by emphasising the cult of violence. At a big fascist rally at Olympia in 1934, brutal behaviour by Blackshirt bodyguards against left-wing hecklers caused a lot of bad publicity; Lord Rothermere stopped supporting Mosley. Moreover, in the same year, the beginnings of economic recovery ended the air of desperate economic crisis that was essential to winning supporters from the traditional and more moderate parties.

BUF membership dropped to 5000 by the end of 1935. In 1936, the government introduced the **Public Order Act** to restrict demonstrations and street fighting. As war approached in the late 1930s, Mosley's pro-Nazi stance alienated even more supporters. Mosley was interned as an enemy alien during the Second World War but by then he was an insignificant figure.

CONCLUSION

Apart from specific events and personalities, there were many reasons why extremism, either Left or Right, failed to make a breakthrough in Britain during the 1930s.

- The economic crisis was not bad enough for long enough. The worst of the slump only affected certain parts of the country; from 1934, there was a degree of economic recovery.
- Support for the traditional parties remained constant. Even at its lowest point in 1931, the Labour Party kept its core voting support. The Conservative Party had a powerful position within the National Government and there was little temptation for Conservative voters to switch to the BUF.
- Political violence turned away more people than it attracted. Mosley never really recovered from the adverse public reaction to the well-publicised violence at his Olympia rally in 1934.
- The National Government took effective action against extremist parties through measures such as the Public Order Act.
- There was considerable **social stability** even in those areas badly hit by the Depression. Crime figures stayed low; the cinema was popular.
- Perhaps, above all, there was no sense of national humiliation in Britain, as there was in 1920s Italy or 1930s Germany. Britain had its monarchy and the empire, and the sense of being a great power in the world.

KEY QUOTE

Social stability George Orwell once claimed that 'Britain was saved from social revolution by fish-and-chip shops, the cinema and the football pools'.

SUMMARY QUESTIONS

1. How badly weakened was the Labour Party after the disasters of 1931?

2. Why did political extremism in Britain fail?

3. How far was stability and economic recovery in Britain in the 1930s due to the actions of the National Government?

CHAPTER 3

How did Britain become involved in the Second World War?

THE ORIGINS OF APPEASEMENT

After 1918, the First World War was often referred to as 'the war to end all wars'. British foreign policy was dedicated to maintaining peace and holding on to the empire. There was also a widespread feeling in the 1920s that the treatment of Germany at the post-war peace settlement had been unfair and unwise; many felt that enforcing the **Treaty of Versailles** was not sufficient reason to begin another major war. Another factor was anti-communism. **The emergence of the Soviet Union** was an unwelcome and frightening development and there were those in Britain who regarded Germany not as an enemy but as a natural ally against the communist threat.

Between 1933 and 1936, the issues of British foreign policy became urgent.

- Hitler came to power in Germany in 1933 and immediately began to build up Germany's armed forces, secretly at first but then openly from 1935.
- Mussolini launched the Italian **invasion of Abyssinia** in 1935, seeking to build an Italian empire in east Africa and laying down a fascist challenge to the League of Nations and the western democracies.
- In 1936, France decided to do nothing when Hitler ignored the terms of the Treaty of Versailles and sent German troops to reoccupy the Rhineland.
- Later, in 1936, the Spanish Civil War began, with the right-wing forces of General Franco supported by Hitler and Mussolini, but with no serious attempt by Britain and France to defend the democratic Spanish Republic. The fact that Stalin *did* send aid to oppose Franco only raised fears of the spread of communism.

Prime Minister Stanley Baldwin was instinctively on the side of the policy that came to be known as appeasement. He was a natural conciliator. He was also from the generation that had the sharpest memories of the First

KEY TREATY

Treaty of Versailles (1919) was the most important of the six treaties signed between 1919 and 1923. German resentment against this 'dictated peace' helped Hitler to gain support. The fact that many in Britain and France had doubts about whether Versailles was unfair or unworkable was one of the elements in appeasement.

KEY EVENTS

The emergence of the Soviet Union The Bolshevik Revolution and Red Army victories in the Civil War in Russia led to the establishment of the Soviet Union as the first Communist state by 1923. It was feared that the USSR would spread revolution and Communist subversion into the western democracies. Anti-communism was a key factor in appeasement.

Invasion of Abyssinia Mussolini invaded Abyssinia in 1935. His success demonstrated the weakness of the League of Nations, and of Britain and France. Along with the Spanish Civil War, it led many left-wingers to oppose the seemingly weak policies of the government.

World War; he had a particular fear of the new technologies of warfare and became famous for saying 'the bomber would always get through'. By 1937, appeasement was already an established policy. Opponents of the policy were on the margins of British politics – on the left wing of the Labour Party, or in the small group that supported Churchill.

NEVILLE CHAMBERLAIN AND THE ROAD TO WAR, 1937–40

Chamberlain did not invent appeasement; however, he came to be *the* politician associated with it. He took personal control of British foreign policy and became the key figure in negotiations with Hitler, especially in the summer of 1938 (even though France was the main military power in Europe). As a result the failure of appeasement remains the main thing that Chamberlain is associated with, despite his long and distinguished career in politics.

Chamberlain's legacy of failure may well be an unfair one. There were many solid reasons in favour of appeasement during the 1930s and the policy was popular at the time. Indeed, there is no way of knowing that a different policy would have succeeded (these issues are explored in more depth in the A2 section p. 65–75). However, after the dramatic events of 1940, Chamberlain came to be widely regarded as a failure, in contrast to the heroic image of Churchill.

The high point of appeasement

There were three stages in the story of appeasement and its failure to avoid war. In the first stage, Chamberlain seemed to achieve success in reacting to the Hitler threat.

- In November 1937, Hitler held a secret conference at which he informed the leaders of Germany's armed forces of his plans for war.
- In March 1938, Hitler marched into Austria to enforce the *Anschluss* between Germany and Austria (forbidden by the Treaty of Versailles); Britain and France took no action.
- In August and September 1938, Hitler put immense pressure on Czechoslovakia to give in to German demands for the German-speaking **Sudetenland**.

The view of France Britain's main ally, France, was even more desperate to avoid war, being divided politically and having suffered even worse losses between 1914–18.

KEY EVENT
The *Anschluss* In March 1938, Hitler forced through the union of Austria with the German Reich. The post-war peace treaties specifically forbade this but Britain and France took no action. Hitler's popularity was shown in a referendum in April, when more than 99 per cent of Germans voted 'yes' to the Anschluss.

KEY PLACE
The Sudetenland were the German-speaking territories that were incorporated into Czechoslovakia in 1919-20. In 1937 and 1938, Hitler put on great international pressure to achieve 'self-determination' for the Sudeten Germans, especially after the Anschluss.

A GREAT MEDIATOR

Punch cartoon of October 1938 showing Chamberlain as 'A Great Mediator'.

- On 2 September, the Soviet Union proposed a joint pact between the Russians, the Czechs, the British and the French (France and the Soviet Union had previously made a **treaty to protect the Czechs** in 1935).
- On 15 September , Chamberlain flew to Berchtesgaden in Germany for direct negotiations with Hitler; two weeks later, Chamberlain returned to Germany for further talks at Bad Godesberg. The outcome of the talks was inconclusive.
- One result of the talks between Hitler and Chamberlain was the Four-power Munich Conference on 30 September, at which Britain, France, Germany and Italy agreed terms for the surrender of the Sudetenland. The Czechs were not invited to the conference even though it was their territory being given away. Nor was the Soviet Union invited.
- Chamberlain returned from Munich to a hero's welcome at Heston airport, claiming to have secured 'peace in our time'. There was mass approval of his actions, both in the national press and from almost all political commentators and church leaders.

This was the high point of appeasement. To be fair to Chamberlain and the government, they did not depend completely on making bargains with Hitler. Britain had begun serious rearmament in 1937 and this was stepped up in 1938, especially in aircraft production. Nevertheless, appeasement continued to be Chamberlain's policy.

The end of appeasement

Then, in March 1939, the second stage began.

- Hitler tore up the **Munich Agreement** by invading the rest of Czechoslovakia and occupying Prague. Next Germany made threats against Poland.
- Chamberlain and the French made it clear that they would go to war to defend Poland if Germany attacked.
- In the summer of 1939, a combined British and French military mission was sent to Moscow to discuss **cooperation between the Soviet Union and the Western Powers** against Germany. These talks were suddenly rendered useless when the Nazi–Soviet Pact was announced. Hitler and Stalin had secretly negotiated a non-aggression pact that gave Germany a

free hand to invade Poland and allowed the Soviet Union to take over significant parts of Eastern Europe.

- On 1 September, Germany invaded Poland. On 3 September, Chamberlain reluctantly declared war.

The events of 1939 seemed to prove that Chamberlain's policy had been a complete failure. He could be criticised for gullibility in accepting Hitler's word as truth and because he had not succeeded in making an alliance with the Soviet Union. Many critics said that this was because Chamberlain had moved too slowly; others argued that Chamberlain was so anti-communist he simply had not tried hard enough. Nevertheless, this was not really the end of appeasement nor the end of Chamberlain. There was still a third stage, known as the 'Phoney War'.

The 'Phoney War'

Britain did not intend an immediate military war against Germany in 1939. Britain and France could not do anything to save Poland from being defeated in a matter of weeks: they were not prepared to invade Germany from the west. Chamberlain's policy was to wait for Hitler's next move. It seems that he was willing to make another agreement, which is what Hitler wanted.

Thus, apart from naval operations, there was little active fighting in the first few months of the Second World War. The main emphasis was on continued rearmament and on strengthening air defences. Winston Churchill returned to government to take command of the navy.

In April 1940, Germany launched its war in the west, attacking Denmark and Holland. A British plan to seize the ports of western Norway went badly wrong and threw the government into crisis. On 10 May, Germany then invaded Belgium and France, winning a series of **lightning victories**. British armies became trapped in northern France. Chamberlain then resigned and Churchill replaced him as prime minister.

Even this was not the final end of appeasement: Churchill was committed to fighting but there was no certainty that he could convince the rest of the government to agree with him. The Foreign Secretary, **Lord Halifax**, had nearly been chosen as prime minister in preference to Churchill; the

KEY TERM

Lightning victories or Blitzkrieg this was the name given to the rapid victories of the German army in the European war of 1939 - 40, based on the principles of speed and the integration between armoured forces and close air support.

KEY PERSON

Lord Halifax (1881-1959) A leading Conservative politician who was Viceroy in India,1926-31, and Foreign Secretary from 1938. He was a key supporter of Chamberlain and appeasement but accepted the appointment of Churchill as prime minister in May 1940; he was then British Ambassador in Washington throughout the war.

Evacuation from Dunkirk
In May 1940, 330 000 British troops were evacuated from the beaches at Dunkirk after the German conquest of France. This was a bad military defeat but was turned into a heroic myth of national defiance by British propaganda.

Churchill as unchallenged leader In the 1930s, Churchill was an unpopular outsider in the Conservative Party. He was able to establish himself as prime minister in 1940 because of the crisis situation and because Halifax accepted he was the right man.

war Cabinet also included Chamberlain. As it became clear that France would surrender, so it seemed obvious to the Halifax–Chamberlain group that Britain would have to face reality and make peace with Hitler.

The decision to continue the war

During five tense days between 24 and 28 May, British troops were successfully **evacuated from Dunkirk** and Churchill was able to overcome the doubters and consolidate his position as **unchallenged leader** of a government. At the end of May 1940, appeasement came to an end and Britain really went to war.

SUMMARY QUESTIONS

1. What were the long and short-term origins of Britain's policy of appeasement?

2. How popular was appeasement with the British people in 1938-39?

3. How and why was Winston Churchill able to become the leader of a united nation in 1940?

CHAPTER 4

What was the impact upon Britain of the Second World War?

THE PHASES OF WAR

After **the fall of France** to Nazi Germany, Britain's war effort went through three distinct phases. In the first phase, from May 1940 to June 1941, Britain was alone. The key was survival. There was no hope of defeating Germany, only to avoid surrender and to make the war last long enough for others to join in. The vital theatres of war were in the air, fending off the German air offensive in the Battle of Britain and the Blitz, and at sea, protecting the convoys in what became the Battle of the Atlantic. Britain's survival owed a lot to Churchill's success in rallying the nation to a united effort and to aid through the **Lend-Lease agreement** after the USA decided that Britain might avoid defeat after all. Then, in 1941, Britain gained powerful allies. First the Soviet Union after Germany invaded her in June 1941 and then the USA when the Japanese attack at Pearl Harbour brought them into the war.

In the second phase, in 1942 and 1943, the European war became a world war. Britain fought alongside the two emerging US and Soviet superpowers until the tide of the war turned against **the Axis**. By the summer of 1943, the USA had the upper hand in the war in the Pacific, the Red Army had won the great battles of Stalingrad and Kursk and was about to drive towards Berlin, and the **U-boats** had been virtually defeated in the Battle of the Atlantic. Hitler's eventual defeat was certain.

In the third phase, from 1943–5, Germany and its allies were crushed by invasion and by mass bombing. In this final phase, Britain was overshadowed by the size and importance of its allies. Just before the end of the war, there was a symbolic meeting of US and Soviet troops at Torgau-on-the-Elbe in the heart of Germany. The Second World War had been won and the Cold War was beginning. The age of the European powers was over.

BRITAIN'S WAR

The Second World War affected Britain in many ways and on many levels. In one sense, the war was a success story. Britain's role in defeating Hitler, especially when Britain fought alone in the crucial period of 1940–1, was a source of national unity and pride. Churchill became a world leader and a national hero. Britain ended the war as a major ally of the USA in the so-called 'special relationship'. Britain had great prestige and took a leading role in the occupation of Germany and in the newly formed United Nations.

In other respects, Britain was badly damaged by the war. There was considerable damage to the nation's infrastructure as a result of enemy bombing. The war was hugely expensive and caused massive increases in government borrowing. Reconstruction after the war would be an extremely long and difficult task. Beyond the economic damage, there was also the question of Britain's ability to continue as a world power. After the Japanese armies overran British colonies in Asia in 1942, **colonial independence movements** were much strengthened. The Second World War intensified a process that had already begun after the First World War and pointed in the direction of de-colonisation.

It might be true to say that the economic and military impact of the war left Britain in the same situation as a defeated nation but with the illusions of victory.

DID THE SECOND WORLD WAR CAUSE A SOCIAL REVOLUTION IN BRITAIN?

The war not only affected Britain's economic strength and its imperial role, it also had a huge impact upon British society. The key question is whether the effects of the war were deep and lasting – a 'social revolution' or a time of intense short-term change due to the exceptional circumstances of wartime, after which British society mostly returned to normal.

- **Shared experiences.** The war caused a massive emphasis on the idea that 'we are all in this together'. The Second World War was a 'People's War', with a universal acceptance of the importance of civilians

---

KEY FACT

Colonial independence movements already existed before the Second World War. After the war, they gained momentum – for example in India, Malaya, and Kenya.

---

fighting on the Home Front. This involved universal acceptance of controls and sacrifices, such as rationing. It also involved the sense of resilience and defiance against the German bombing campaign. The idea of the 'People's War' peaked in 1940–1 during the Blitz. Sharing bomb shelters and going through the experience of the evacuation of children from the inner cities to safer homes elsewhere cut across class barriers. The role of the BBC became central to the war effort and people of all classes habitually listened to the same broadcasts each day.

- **State intervention and direct controls.** The government had considerable special powers during the war. This included conscription, censorship, and the allocation of labour. During the years of the war, people became accustomed to greater state intervention in the economy and in daily life. Planning came to be regarded as beneficial and effective.

- **Propaganda.** The war produced a huge amount of official and unofficial propaganda, much of it aimed at fostering a spirit of national unity. There was intensive use of the radio, both through news and light entertainment. There was a highly effective poster campaign to get across messages such as *Dig for Victory* and *Careless Talk Costs Lives*.

- **Social mobility.** The war took thousands of people out of the lives they had previously known. Young men called into the armed forces found themselves in situations they could never have experienced previously and mixing with a cross-section of society. Many unmarried girls in employment or service found themselves living away from home in circumstances they would never have before thought possible. The war brought together a range of people from different class backgrounds and different regions.

- **Americanisation.** Through light entertainment and especially through the arrival in England of thousands of US servicemen, US influences had a big effect on British society. This trend was already there in the 1930s due to Hollywood films, but the war greatly intensified it.

- **Changed roles for women.** The war caused a massive increase in the employment of women – in factories, in clerical jobs and in uniform. Girls became **WAAFs,**

KEY THEME

Film and propaganda

The film industry became almost an arm of the propaganda machine and produced many feature films, such as *In Which We Serve* and *Went the day well*, with the theme of national unity and presenting a favourable image of the working classes.

WAAFs the Women's Auxiliary Air Force
Women's role in the Air Force included desk jobs, photographic analysis and flying transport aircraft.

Stenographers Shorthand typists. A stenograph is a machine for writing shorthand, operated by keyboard.

Fitters were mechanics maintaining fighter and bomber aircraft.

ATS the women serving the Army Transport Service.

WRNS or WRENS were the Women's Royal Navy Service. Many 'Wrens' performed vital roles such as tracking the U-boat threat to Allied convoys.

Land Girls, **stenographers**, and drivers of everything from jeeps to cranes. Many married women had to take on heavy responsibilities because the men were away. The rapid movement of wartime led to much greater freedom in sexual relationships; there was a sharp increase in the divorce rate as a result of the war.

- **Changed attitudes.** The war caused many Britons to look differently at recent history. Communism seemed different when Britain was allied to the Soviet Union (as she was from 1941). The 'Hungry Thirties' became fixed in memory as an awful time of hardship and social division, never to be repeated. The whole idea of building a better post-war society was widely accepted.

The case for continuity

- **Reality was different from the propaganda myths.** The idea of shared experience was not always true. Middle-class people tended to live away from the main centres of the bombing raids; those with money could always get round the rationing restrictions. Nor was it always true that people rallied to the needs of the community. There were many cases of looting and petty thieving (blackout and bomb damage provided ideal conditions). When dignitaries like Churchill or the Queen visited bomb-damaged areas, crowds were often sullen or hostile.

- **Most of the effects of change were temporary.** Many women gave up their jobs at the end of the war, either because they wished to or were forced to. Class loyalties ran deep and stayed much the same as they had before the war.

- **War service did more to reinforce class divisions than to break them down.** In real life and even in the world of cosy propaganda films, the armed forces were organised on class lines. Working-class and regional accents belonged to the **fitters**, not to the pilots, to privates but not officers. Working-class girls ended up in the **ATS**, whereas bourgeois girls joined the **WRNS** or staffed the code-breaking machines at Bletchley Park. The social mobility of the war did more to move people from place to place than to cross class barriers.

It is clear that much of the so-called 'People's War' was indeed myth. It is true that the exceptional conditions of war put people into exceptional personal circumstances but once the war was over life returned to normal. Nevertheless, it is also impossible to avoid the fact that many lives *were* changed. Indeed, the basis for the introduction of the Welfare State after the war was the change in social attitudes that made the **Beveridge Plan** so popular when it was launched during the war. Many people genuinely believed, and *wanted* to believe, that there had been fundamental social change.

HOW EFFECTIVE A WAR LEADER WAS WINSTON CHURCHILL?

When Churchill became prime minister in May 1940, Britain's military position was bad and getting worse. The fall of France was already in progress; Britain had no other significant ally and was about to face the full weight of Hitler's war machine. Churchill's leadership of Britain's war effort was at its most vital in 1940 and 1941 during Britain's 'Finest Hour'; it was almost as important in 1942 and 1943, when Churchill was part of the so-called 'Big Three' alongside **Franklin Roosevelt** and Stalin in the Grand Alliance. In 1944 and 1945, despite his huge personal prestige, Churchill began to be overshadowed by the two emerging superpowers although he continued to play an important part in the preparations for the post-war world.

Rallying Britain to war, 1940–1

From May 1940 until December 1941, when the USA entered the war after the attack on Pearl Harbour, Britain was virtually alone. It was in this period that Churchill made his greatest contribution. Ironically, it was by no means certain in May 1940 that Churchill would be able to establish himself in power. He had always had a stormy relationship with the Conservative Party and many regarded him as a maverick. He had been wrong on most of the big issues of the 1930s, including India and the abdication of Edward VIII. He was 65 years old in 1940 and would have regarded his career up to then as a personal failure. In May 1940, it was a great achievement to make himself

Winston Churchill.

The evidence for and against Churchill as a great war leader

FOR	AGAINST
Winning the battle inside the Conservative Party for carrying on with the war against Germany.	He made many strategic mistakes, such as Norway in 1940, or the loss of Singapore in 1942.
Choosing a broad-based and effective coalition Cabinet.	Propaganda myths concealed many truths about public opinion.
Giving an inspiring lead and fostering a sense of national unity.	In 1942, he had to survive a 'no confidence' vote in Parliament.
Handling important and difficult allies such as Stalin, President Roosevelt and de Gaulle.	His handling of the allies can be criticised; for example, in allowing himself to be outmanoeuvred by Stalin.
Decisive action in choosing and backing key military commanders.	
Exploiting successfully the strengths of British scientists and code breakers.	He placed too much reliance on mass bombing as a tactic of war thereby causing needless loss of life.

KEY PERSON

de Gaulle (1890-1970) de Gaulle became leader of the 'Free French' forces who were carrying on with the war after the Fall of France. Prickly and vain, he was fiercely disliked by Roosevelt, and often a headache for Churchill. He became Head of State in France after the Liberation in 1944.

unchallenged leader of the government, partly by luck (he had no way of knowing that Hitler would allow the British army to escape at Dunkirk) and partly by sheer force of personality.

Harnessing the war spirit

Churchill's second great achievement was to rally public opinion and create a sense of national unity. He was a propaganda genius who knew how to put across the essential message. Churchill was not only able to do this with the public at large; he also had a dramatic effect on commanders of the armed forces and on government bureaucrats. He was also able to appoint a highly effective war Cabinet, making full use of former political opponents. He exploited fully the talents of Labour politicians such as **Ernest Bevin** and **Hugh Dalton**; in turn, they hugely admired him. It is doubtful if any other Conservative leader could have managed this.

Forming alliances

Churchill's third and ultimate achievement was to gain the allies that could enable Britain to win the war. The British could not win the war in 1940–1, but they could **make the war last long enough** until other powers joined. Even before Pearl Harbour, Churchill was able to establish the basis of a future alliance with Franklin Roosevelt. From December 1941, the Anglo–American alliance was the basis of Britain's whole war effort. (There is a sample essay on Churchill and Britain's allies in the Assessment Section, page 59.)

In 1942 and 1943, Churchill was at the heart of the Grand Alliance, sharing in the big strategic decisions. There were many successes and many failures. Successes included the victories in North Africa, the defence of the Atlantic convoys against the U-boats, the Normandy invasion in 1944, and the brilliant management of the secret war of scientific weapons and code breaking. Failures included the early disasters in the war in the Far East, especially the loss of Britain's biggest battleships, and the fall of Singapore. Historians still disagree about the effectiveness of the mass bombing of Germany between 1942 and 1945.

From the middle of 1943, it became clear that Britain was going to be overshadowed as a great power by the US and Soviet superpowers. Churchill had less and less decisive influence, though his massive personal prestige tended to hide the fact. When he was voted out of power in 1945, it was a shock to many. Churchill was taking a shower when the confirmation of the election defeat came through. His manservant expressed sympathy and surprise that an ungrateful public could have voted in such a way. 'That's democracy,' snapped Churchill, 'hand me my towel.'

Why did Labour win a landslide victory in 1945?

The Labour landslide in the general election of 1945 was a great surprise. Many Tory supporters simply could not believe that Winston Churchill would be rejected at the polls in the moment of victory. Many Labour voters hoped they might win but were actually convinced deep down that they would lose. In fact, there were many underlying reasons why a Labour victory was likely in 1945.

REASONS FOR VOTING LABOUR IN 1945

Some of these reasons pre-dated the war (see pages 13–24). The Labour Party had recovered after the disaster of 1931 that saw the Labour government collapse. It had also protected its supporters from potential political rivals like the BUF or the communists. In the late 1930s, Labour politicians who attacked the 'Guilty Men' of appeasement had taken a political position that would later give them great credibility; on the other hand, the Conservative Party was associated in voters' minds with Chamberlain and appeasement.

However, the most important factors took effect between 1940 and 1945.

- The Second World War, the so-called 'People's War', led to fundamental changes in British society and hence in political attitudes. The war increased the sense of shared experience and made state intervention and planning seem a good idea.

- The wartime coalition government gave leading figures in the Labour Party a huge opportunity to prove themselves on the national stage. The key Conservatives in the coalition, Churchill and **Eden**, were deeply involved in wartime diplomacy; the key Labour figures, Attlee, **Morrison** and Ernest Bevin, were responsible for the Home Front and therefore much in the public eye.
- Wartime propaganda and social policy emphasised togetherness and national unity; this fitted well with socialist philosophy. The Beveridge Plan (page 47) and the proposals for a Welfare State became very popular from 1942; the Labour Party was trusted to be fully behind this, whereas some Conservatives, including Churchill, were seen as lukewarm.
- Involvement in the wartime coalition proved Labour politicians patriotic as well as reliable. This made it hard for Conservatives to attack them for being 'unpatriotic', as had often happened in the past (because of the connections of many Labour MPs to pacifism and international socialism). Britain's wartime alliance with the Soviet Union from 1941 onwards also made international socialism more respectable.
- The attitude of the national press during the war, for example, the influential cartoons of David Low in the *Evening Standard*, was in favour of moving forward to a better post-war world, leaving the grim memories of the 1930s in the past.

The 1945 election campaign

By the end of the war in 1945, public perceptions of the Labour Party had changed. Labour entered the election campaign with better chances of success than ever before. There were also several key factors in the actual campaign that worked in favour of Labour and against the Conservatives.

- **Holding an election so soon after the end of the war.** The Conservative Party had always had the advantage in previous elections of a well-oiled 'party machine', run by election agents and well-organised volunteers. In 1945, under unusual circumstances and with many people still in uniform, this machine was unable to function as it usually did.

- **Complacency.** Many Conservatives believed a grateful nation would automatically 'thank' Churchill; they underrated Labour's chances.
- **The Labour election manifesto.** This was far more forward-looking and appealing than the Conservative manifesto.
- **Winston Churchill.** Churchill was not as big an asset as many might have expected. Many voters associated him with the nation as a whole, not with the Conservative Party. He was also seen as a war leader, not the right man for peacetime reconstruction. A large percentage of armed service personnel voted Labour.
- **Campaign errors.** Churchill lost many votes through his **Gestapo speech** early in the campaign, when he unwisely tried to scare voters with the idea that a Labour government would mean totalitarian state control and a secret police.

It is difficult to believe that the 1945 electoral campaign could have decided the outcome of the election, though it might have increased the margin of victory. Labour's landslide was by such a decisive margin that it was almost certainly a foregone conclusion before electioneering even started. Even so, it should not be forgotten that, at the

KEY FACT

Gestapo Speech In a radio broadcast in June 1945, Churchill warned voters that any Socialist government would need to use 'some kind of secret police or Gestapo'. Clem Atlee's calm and effective response to this claim did much to boost support for Labour.

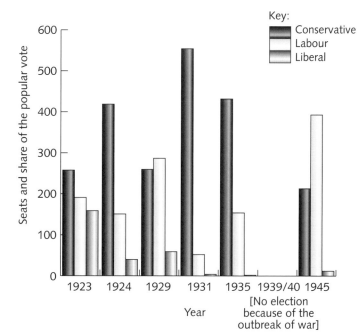

General election results, 1923–45.

time, many people – both delighted Labour supporters and shocked Conservatives – were astonished by the result.

SUMMARY QUESTIONS

1. How important was the personal contribution of Winston Churchill to Britain's war effort in 1940-45?

2. To what extent did the Second World War bring about a 'social revolution' in Britain?

3. How significant was the role of Labour politicians in the wartime coalition government?

4. How far did the outcome of the 1945 election reflect fundamental social change in Britain during the war?

5. How significant was the experience of Labour politicians in the wartime coalition government in increasing electoral support for Labour by 1945?

6. To what extent did the British people reject Churchill and the Conservatives in 1945?

KEY THEME

Long term economic decline Britain's economic crisis was not only due to the burdens of the war. Many areas of British industry had been struggling against long-term decline since the 1920s and had been badly hit by the Depression in the Thirties. In some industries, like shipbuilding and steel, the war had actually provided a significant boost after the dark days of the Thirties; however, it was likely that adverse long-term trends would take effect again after the war.

KEY EVENT

Ending of the Lend-Lease arrangements The sudden ending of Lend-Lease showed that the USA was an economic rival as well as a military ally. The Americans did not realize how economically weak Britain was until the crisis of February 1947.

CHAPTER 5

Britain, 1945–64

BRITAIN IN 1945

The state of the post-war economy

Britain was in a contradictory position at the end of the Second World War. Unlike continental Europe, Britain had not been under occupation. Outwardly, there was the image of a victorious nation, one of the 'Big Three' that had won the war and would now dominate the post-war world. This sense of victory had a deep influence on British policy in foreign and imperial affairs.

On the other hand, Britain faced a desperate economic and financial situation in 1945. Six years of war had drained Britain's financial reserves. Wartime debts had been running at £70 million per day. Fighting the war alone in 1940–1 had placed Britain in a state of almost total dependence on the USA. Many of Britain's traditional export markets had been dislocated; this made the sudden **ending of the Lend-Lease arrangements** in August 1945 a terrible blow.

Foreign policy ambitions

There was a similar situation in foreign and imperial affairs. Before the war, Britain's control of the empire had come under great pressure, especially in India and the Middle East. After 1945, the world was dominated by two anti-colonial superpowers. It was inevitable that colonial independence movements would therefore be strengthened.

The new Attlee government was thus pulled in contradictory directions.

- The need for post-war reconstruction and economic recovery: large parts of the Labour Party were eager for nationalisation, post-war planning and the Welfare State, all of which depended on economic recovery.
- The drive, strongly influenced by Ernest Bevin, to maintain Britain's role as a world power. This meant keeping up military commitments, defending the empire and taking a leading role in the Cold War as a

key ally of the USA (in the so-called 'special relationship'). It also meant Britain developing its own independent nuclear weapons programme. All these commitments meant huge costs and were bound to increase the strain on Britain's over-burdened economy.

How could it be possible to bring about economic recovery after the disasters of the 1930s and the huge costs of the Second World War, to finance a new and better society through the Welfare State, and to continue Britain's role as a world power, all at the same time?

HOW WELL DID BRITAIN RECOVER FROM THE WAR IN THE YEARS 1945–51?

The popularity of the Labour government in 1945

The new Labour government was well equipped to take on its tasks in 1945. It had a huge parliamentary majority, the first time any Labour government had ever had such an outright majority. It also had massive public support growing out of the war and the idea of the Welfare State was popular.

The Labour Cabinet was a strong team. Attlee himself proved a very capable prime minister. Other Labour leaders had achieved both experience and public respect during the war. Hugh Dalton, Herbert Morrison and most of all the new Foreign Secretary Ernest Bevin, had all been successful and respected figures in the wartime coalition. A large number of talented politicians, including **Harold Wilson**, had been elected in the 1945 landslide. The old charge that Labour was fundamentally left wing, unpatriotic and unreliable now seemed ridiculous.

There were other favourable factors. The war had produced full employment, something that continued for a generation after 1945. The trade unions were greatly strengthened by the war and had established for a while a cooperative relationship with government. Moreover, the Labour Party had never before been treated with such broad acceptance and approval by most of the national press.

Economic crisis

At first, the government underestimated the difficulties in achieving economic recovery. In 1945, Britain negotiated

Public support of the war
Wartime propaganda had fostered a strong sense of unity and a determination to build a better world. The idea of a 'People's War' may have been a myth; nevertheless, it was a powerful one, symbolised by the well-known Low cartoons during and after the war (see page 53 for an example of a Low cartoon).

Harold Wilson (1916-1995) Wilson became a Labour MP in 1945. He was the youngest cabinet minister for 150 years. He was a supporter of Aneurin Bevan in the clash with Gaitskell in 1951. He became leader of the Labour party in 1963 and prime minister in 1964.

loans from the USA and Canada totalling more than $5000 million. The Chancellor, Hugh Dalton, was optimistic about the economic prospects during 1946. There was full employment and the US loans would come into operation from July. Then the exceptionally hard winter of 1947 revealed the true depths of Britain's economic situation: there was a fuel crisis, a dollar crisis, and a crisis of expenditure on foreign commitments.

The fuel crisis. This was caused by the worst winter to hit Britain since 1881. Coal dumps froze, transport was paralysed and the electricity supply was drastically cut. Industry had to cut back and there was severe temporary unemployment. The minister responsible, **Emanuel Shinwell**, became a scapegoat: the slogan 'Shiver with Shinwell' was very popular with critics of the government. Hugh Dalton was forced to resign (over a different issue) and was replaced as Chancellor by **Stafford Cripps**. It was Cripps who became identified with the term 'austerity' as the government imposed tight restrictions on the economy – including the rationing of bread, which had not been rationed during the war.

The dollar crisis of 1947. This was triggered by the terms of the US loan: it was a condition of the loan that the pound sterling would be convertible with the US dollar. When this came into effect in July 1947, there was an immediate run on the pound (this was a heavy selling of the pound sterling on the international money markets that led to **devaluation** of the pound in 1949) that used up considerable amounts of the US loan. It became essential to halt convertibility. Not long afterwards, in 1949, it was decided to devalue the pound. The exchange rate fell from $4.03 to $2.80, a devaluation of 30 per cent.

The expenditure crisis. This was partly caused by economic issues at home: plans for the nationalisation of key industries and the introduction of the Welfare State were expensive. Foreign commitments were also huge:

- spending on the British occupation zone in Germany was about £234 million
- Britain was involved in administering Palestine
- Britain was providing aid to Greece and Turkey.

By the summer of 1947, there was a serious balance of payments problem. The 1946 US loan had almost run out. These economic weaknesses caused the government to turn to the USA again. In February 1947, Washington was informed that Britain would pull out of Greece and Turkey within six weeks. This was a big surprise to the Americans; they had overrated Britain's economic strength. This realisation was a key influence on the US decision to launch the **Marshall Plan**.

From austerity to growth

The 1947 economic crisis did not mean that the British economy was on the point of collapse. Indeed, 1947 was the year when the economy began a slow recovery from austerity to growth. There were several aspects to this recovery.

- Marshall Aid. From 1948, Britain received more than $1250 million in aid from the USA, more than any other European country except France.
- The success of Cripps's austerity programme: in cutting costs, reducing imports and avoiding inflation.
- A gradual recovery in British exports: by 1950, exports were 75 per cent higher than before the war.

By 1948, the economy was stable enough for the government to announce a 'bonfire of controls'. Rationing was removed from many items and several other direct controls over the allocation of labour were lifted. By this time, too, the government had carried through most of its plans for **nationalisation**.

By 1950, the economy had weathered the immediate crisis and was poised to embark on the lengthy prosperity of the post-war period. Nationalisation was mostly completed and the Welfare State was in place. The start of the **Korean War** (June 1950) put the economy back under pressure (it caused a split within the government over welfare spending) but the Labour government could claim to have achieved most of its objectives on the domestic front.

KEY TERM

Marshall Plan George Marshall was the American secretary of state in 1947. When it was realized how urgent the economic crisis was in Britain and western Europe, Marshall designed a scheme for massive financial aid.

KEY EVENT

Nationalisation The Bank of England was nationalised in 1946 followed by coal in 1947, the railways and the electricity industry in 1948 and gas in 1949. The last, most difficult nationalisation was iron and steel in 1951.

Korean War In 1950, forces from Communist North Korea invaded the South. Later, these forces were supported by Communist China. Forces (mostly American and British) were sent on behalf of the United Nations to defend South Korea. The war was ended by a compromise peace in 1954.

HOW SUCCESSFULLY DID THE ATTLEE GOVERNMENT MAINTAIN BRITAIN'S WORLD ROLE?

It might have been expected that the approach of the Labour government to foreign affairs would differ considerably from that of the Conservatives. Labour was traditionally less enthusiastic about the empire than, for example, a Tory government under Churchill would have been. The left wing of the Labour Party was generally sympathetic to the Soviet Union and suspicious about world domination by the USA. Despite this the Attlee government took a traditional line in most aspects of foreign policy. Palestine and India were granted independence in 1947 but there was no rush to dismantle the empire as a whole. Britain remained committed to maintaining its position as a world power.

The role of Ernest Bevin

The key personality of the new government was the Foreign Secretary, Ernest Bevin. Those Labour politicians who had served in the wartime coalition were proud of Britain's role in defeating Hitler, but it was Bevin who was most determined to follow in Churchill's footsteps. Bevin was a tough character from the right wing of the party. He had fought countless battles against the Left in the 1930s. He was absolutely convinced that communism was a danger and that it was vital to maintain US involvement with Western Europe. Bevin also had a very strong position in the Labour Cabinet – the government was based on the alliance between Bevin and Attlee. Labour's foreign policy after 1945 was mostly Bevin's policy.

Until 1947, it was not clear how the Cold War was going to develop or how much Britain might have to scale down foreign commitments because of economic weakness. The key moment was in February 1947 when the government urgently informed the USA that Britain would be pulling out of Greece and Turkey. For the first time, the US government realised that the threat of economic collapse in Britain and Western Europe was serious.

Bevin was deeply committed to the containment of communism.

- He was behind the scheme for a joint currency for the USA and British zones of occupation.
- He was a firm ally of the USA when supporting West Berlin during the **Berlin Blockade**.
- He took the lead during the formation of the **Brussels Pact** in 1948, which led to the establishment of the North Atlantic Treaty Organisation (NATO) in 1949.

The Empire

In Imperial affairs, Attlee's government attempted a compromise policy, allowing for more colonial self-government and moving towards a liberal multiracial Commonwealth. This policy had mixed success. India did achieve independence in 1947, followed by Burma and Ceylon (Sri Lanka) in 1948. However, the process of leaving India was confused and complicated: there were many thousands of deaths in racial community violence after British withdrawal. Efforts to 'make the empire pay' through economic development in Africa and elsewhere proved very unsuccessful.

Criticisms of Labour's foreign policy, 1945–51

Labour's policies, and the role of Bevin, have been criticised on several grounds since 1951.

- The left wing of the Party blamed Bevin for intensifying the Cold War: for being too pro-American and missing the opportunity to maintain good relations with the Soviet Union in the post-war period.
- Bevin was attacked for Foreign Office failures over the handling of the Palestine issue. Attlee's government was accused of following an anti-Jewish policy, and of failing to keep control of security issues before Britain was forced to pull out in 1947.
- The secret decision of the Cabinet to develop Britain's own nuclear weapons led to vast government spending and to lasting divisions within the Labour Party.
- It has been claimed that British foreign policy continued to be based on unrealistic illusions. These illusions were

KEY EVENT

Berlin Blockade In 1945 Berlin was liberated by Soviet armies but control of the city was shared by the four occupying powers. In 1948, Stalin cut off all western access to the city of west Berlin in an attempt to ensure Soviet control. This 'blockade' led to the Berlin airlift which kept west Berlin supplied from the air until Stalin backed down in 1949.

KEY TREATY

Brussels Pact In 1948, Ernest Bevin played a key part in forming an anti-communist alliance between Britain, the USA and western Europe. A meeting in Brussels prepared the way for the NATO alliance to be formed in 1949.

not blown away until the **Suez Crisis** in 1956, and maybe not even then.

Nevertheless, there is much evidence to claim that Labour's foreign policies were successful. Indeed, these policies were mostly continued after 1951 without major changes by later Conservative governments.

HOW EFFECTIVELY WAS THE WELFARE STATE ESTABLISHED?

The keystone of Labour's policies in 1945 was the setting up of the Welfare State. This was the biggest practical move to reduce poverty. Possibly the key reason why so many people had voted Labour in the general election was the belief that Labour could be trusted with the implementation of the Beveridge Plan.

The Beveridge Report, 1942

The idea of comprehensive social reform came to the fore during the war, almost precisely at the time when it seemed certain that defeat would be avoided. In December 1942, the Beveridge Report outlined the three key principles for a system of social security:

- family allowances
- a comprehensive national health service
- full employment.

This was not a specifically Labour scheme. **William Beveridge** was a Liberal, not a socialist, and the wartime government as a whole commissioned his report. Nor did the Beveridge Report offer a blueprint for starting from scratch. Britain already had a range of welfare services before 1939, for example the wartime government provided free school meals and milk. However, the Beveridge proposals were close to plans current in the Labour Party, thus Labour became associated with its core ideas. The big difference between Beveridge and the Labour Party is that Beveridge did not believe in wholesale state planning; Labour, did.

On publication, the Beveridge Report had an inspiring effect, especially because it promised to do away with the two most hated features of the 1930s: unemployment and the Means Test. The wartime government began planning for post-war reconstruction, which went against the wishes of Churchill (preoccupied with winning the war) and of the Treasury (worried about the cost).

Before the end of the war, several steps were taken towards the establishment of the aims of the report. A White Paper on employment policy was issued in 1944, outlining the commitment to high and stable employment. In the same year, **R.A. Butler's Education Act** was passed. In 1945, after Labour had broken away from the wartime coalition to fight the general election, the caretaker Conservative government passed the **Family Allowance Act**. Since there was a great deal of public enthusiasm and press support for social reform, the nation was prepared for the implementation of the Beveridge Report well before Attlee's Labour government came to power.

Between 1945 and 1948, the building blocks of the Welfare State were put in place:

- the National Health Service Act, 1946
- the National Insurance Act, 1946
- the National Assistance Act, 1948 (for those outside national insurance)
- the Town and Country Planning Act, 1947.

The Beveridge Plan was so popular that few politicians would have dared to oppose it openly. Nevertheless, there was opposition.

- Some right-wing Conservatives opposed it on the grounds of the cost of universal provision. (It is often wrongly stated that Churchill was flatly against the Beveridge Plan: he was sceptical of parts but not against it.)
- Some on the Labour Left opposed it because it did not go far enough: in addition to the NHS they wanted to nationalise all the hospitals and to make doctors into salaried civil servants.

Aneurin Bevan and the NHS

The most important, most costly and most difficult part of the Welfare State was the National Health Service (NHS). **Aneurin Bevan** was the minister given the task of pushing through the National Health Service Act. He was

R. A. Butler (1902-1982) 'Rab' Butler was an experienced Conservative politician, who was a minister in the National Government 1932-40 and in the wartime coalition. He masterminded the Education Act of 1944. He was a key figure in rebuilding the Conservatives after the 1945 defeat. Later, he came very close to being prime minister, both in 1957 and in 1963.

Education Act, 1944 this provided secondary education for all up to the age of 15 in a system of grammar schools, secondary modern schools and technical high schools.

Family Allowance Act, 1945 this provided mothers with direct state payments to support their young children.

Aneurin Bevan (1897-1960) 'Nye' Bevan was a South Wales miner who became the leading figure on the left wing of the Labour Party. As Minister of Health in the Attlee government, he pushed through the establishment of the National Health Service. In 1951, Bevan resigned from the Cabinet after a clash with the Chancellor Hugh Gaitskell. In 1950s, the 'Bevanite left' was frequently in conflict with the party leadership.

a controversial left-winger who had been expelled from the Labour Party in 1939 and was nearly expelled again in 1944. His appointment as Minister of Health was a red rag to the British Medical Association (BMA) who thought he would be a 'vulgar agitator'. In fact, Bevan turned out to be a skilful negotiator and a realist.

Bevan knew that it would be almost impossible to get the BMA to agree to nationalised hospitals. He settled for a system based on payments per patient: this allowed doctors to combine private practice with working for the NHS.

It took a long time to reach an agreement. In February 1948, 90 per cent of doctors were **hostile to the NHS**. Officially, Conservative politicians were in favour of the scheme; however, many of them were happy to exploit the doctors' opposition. Bevan had to make an explicit declaration that there would be no salaried service before the doctors would consent. By the end of 1948, 93 per cent of all patients were enrolled in the NHS, with 90 per cent of doctors signed up.

DOTHEBOYS HALL
"It still tastes awful."

Cartoon about Aneurin Bevan and the NHS – Aneurin Bevan is spoonfeeding Joe Public medicine.

Consolidation of the Welfare State

Between 1942 and 1948, the Welfare State took shape. After 1948, it was a question of consolidation: politically, the main battles had been won.

The Conservatives would maintain the Welfare State after 1945, constantly declaring that the NHS was 'safe in their hands'. However, there were still battles being fought inside the Labour Party. Left-wing voices, such as the Socialist Medical Association, were disappointed that Bevan had compromised; they had wanted the full nationalisation of hospitals. There were other issues, too, such as education, over which the Left felt that Attlee's government had not been socialist enough; they felt great opportunities to achieve real equality had been missed.

The biggest controversies surrounding the Welfare State were those regarding finance. When Bevan began the battle to carry through the NHS in 1946 and 1947, he was lucky to have firm support from the Chancellor, Hugh Dalton. When the scheme became manifest in 1948, it proved to be less expensive than some critics had feared. However, from 1950, Bevan found himself in conflict with the new Chancellor, **Hugh Gaitskell**, who wanted to curb spending. The start of the Korean War in June 1950 put government finances under severe pressure. This was the point at which a furious row began between Gaitskell, who proposed bringing in prescription charges, and Bevan, who was totally opposed to doing so.

The result of the Bevan–Gaitskell split was significant: Bevan lost the struggle in Cabinet and resigned, Labour lost one of their star performers. Even worse, the split helped to bring about a premature election in 1951 that put Labour out of power. It also began a lengthy and divisive battle between Gaitskell and the Bevanites that weakened the Labour Party throughout the 1950s.

In spite of being driven to resign in 1951, Bevan was successful in bringing the NHS into being. Labour's welfare policies in general were successful and continued by governments of both parties after 1951. Whether the Attlee legacy as a whole was beneficial to the country is discussed in A2 section 1 (page 76).

KEY PERSON

Hugh Gaitskell (1906-1963) a leading figure on the Right wing of the Labour Party, Gaitskell was secretary to Hugh Dalton during the war and became an MP in 1945. He succeeded Stafford Cripps as Chancellor in 1950 and clashed with Nye Bevan in 1951. He was leader of the Labour Party from 1955 to 1963, often in bitter conflict with the Left.

KEY EVENTS

The elections of 1950 and 1951

February 1950

Conservative	298
Labour	315
Liberals	9

February 1951

Conservative	321
Labour	295
Liberals	6

KEY PERSON

Lord Woolton (1883-1964) a businessman who was made Minister of Food in the wartime coalition. He became a Conservative MP in 1945 and played a key role in re-organising the Conservative Party to enable it to recover from its election defeat.

WHY DID LABOUR LOSE POWER IN 1951?

The Labour Party won a narrow victory in the 1950 general election. Even though the Labour majority was much reduced, there were hopes that the achievements of 1945–50 could be consolidated. If the Labour government had been able to remain in power into the 1950s, the government would have benefited from the beginnings of consumer prosperity and the post-war boom. However, the second Attlee government lasted for only twenty months: Attlee called for new elections in October 1951. Labour lost, narrowly, and Churchill came back to power. The key question is why was a Labour government that had achieved so much since 1945 rejected by the voters?

There were a number of factors that might have contributed to Labour's loss of power in 1951.

- The Labour government was associated in many people's minds with the image of Stafford Cripps and his policy of 'austerity' and sacrifices such as rationing and devaluation.
- Many key members of the Cabinet were exhausted or unwell; those like Bevin and Attlee had been working continuously under intense strain since 1940.
- Internal splits, especially the row with Gaitskell that led to Bevan's resignation in 1951, undermined the cohesion of the government.
- The Conservative Party had re-organised effectively under the Party Chairman, **Lord Woolton**, and was once again a powerful and efficient electoral machine (it had not been in the 1945 election).
- The 1951 election came too soon, before the economic prosperity that marked the 1950s was fully apparent.
- As so often before, the 'first-past-the-post' electoral system exaggerated the effects of a relatively small swing of votes away from Labour.
- The continued decline of the Liberals benefited the Conservative Party more than it did Labour.

WHY DID THE CONSERVATIVES DOMINATE BRITISH POLITICS BETWEEN 1951 AND 1964?

Labour's narrow defeat in 1951 led to thirteen long years out of power. The Conservative Party was re-established as the 'natural party of government'.

	Prime Minister	Conservative	Labour	Liberals	Others
1951	Winston Churchill	325	295	6	3
1955	Anthony Eden	344	277	6	3
[1957	Harold Macmillan]				
1959	Harold Macmillan	365	258	6	1
1964	Alec Douglas-Home	304	317	9	–

The Conservatives in power, 1951–64.

Why was the Conservative Party so dominant in the 1950s?

Winston Churchill returned as prime minister from 1951–55 but was no longer the dynamic leader of the war years. He was now very old (when he returned to Downing Street in 1951 he was 76 years old) and was often in very **poor health**. Many in the Party felt that Churchill hung on to power for far too long and that he was too late in handing the prime ministership over to his longstanding successor, Anthony Eden.

Nevertheless, Churchill's government of 1951–5 was broadly successful. The Conservatives were lucky to come to power at the time when the economic prosperity of the long post-war boom was setting in. Although Churchill himself was often inactive, Anthony Eden was a capable and respected figure, able to coordinate government effectively during Churchill's frequent absences. A number of talented ministers, such as R.A Butler and **Harold Macmillan**, carried through social policies that were widely accepted and did not break away from the so-called 'post-war consensus' established by the Attlee governments. Macmillan, for example, had impressive success in increasing the number of houses built.

Meanwhile, the Labour Party continued to suffer from the internal divisions that had emerged during 1950 and 1951. Long before the 1955 general election, it was clear that the Conservative Party would win comfortably.

KEY FACT

Churchill's poor health
When the memoirs of Churchill's doctor, Lord Moran, were published in later years, they caused a sensation by revealing how seriously Churchill had been incapacitated by illness during his last term in office, especially by the effects of a series of strokes.

KEY PERSON

Harold Macmillan (1894-1986) Conservative MP for Stockton-on-Tees 1924-45, he was known for his progressive 'Middle Way' views and was an opponent of appeasement. He was Churchill's representative in North Africa 1942-45. He became Minister of Housing in 1951 and held several other key cabinet posts under Churchill and Eden. He became prime minister in 1957.

Cartoon of the Suez Crisis – by David Low, first published in The Guardian, 16/9/59

When Churchill finally retired in 1955 the new prime minister, Anthony Eden, seemed to inherit a strong position. The long-term prospects were favourable, both politically and economically. Nobody in 1955 would have predicted that Eden would resign in disgrace within two years and it was even more surprising that the cause of Eden's fall should be foreign affairs, the very field area of government for which he was most famous.

THE SUEZ CRISIS

The immediate cause of the Suez fiasco was the rise to power of the nationalist Egyptian leader, **Gamal Abdel Nasser**. The anti-imperialist policies of Nasser were seen as threatening western interests – and especially when he allied himself to the Soviet Union. In 1956, however, the problem was not the Cold War but the fact that Nasser had seized the Suez Canal, which had been controlled by Britain since 1875. Anthony Eden convinced himself that Nasser was another fascist dictator and that 'appeasement' was out of the question; losing the canal was seen as a deadly blow to Britain's economic and strategic position. Eden orchestrated a joint plan with France (and secretly with Israel) to invade Egypt and to seize back the canal.

The use of military force to intervene in Egypt, in October 1956, might have succeeded in military terms. However, Britain was no longer a world power able to act independently. **President Eisenhower** made it plain that the USA would not condone Eden's policy and put heavy US pressure on the British government to pull out. Above all, the withdrawal of US trade and financial help had a dangerous effect on the British economy. Eden's Chancellor, Harold Macmillan, who had originally been in favour of the Suez intervention, was insistent that Britain had to pull out. The result was a humiliating failure of British foreign policy.

Eden's position was much worse because of the secret collusion with France and Israel, and the clear impression that he had deliberately misled Parliament about the justification for going to war. The Suez Crisis caused a split within the Conservatives and a storm of protest from other political parties and much of the press. Eden was forced to resign 'on the grounds of ill-health': he was indeed genuinely ill after a botched abdominal operation, but this was only the pretext not the cause of his resignation.

What was the impact upon Britain of the Suez Crisis?

The Suez Crisis of 1956 was a symbolic turning point in the history of post-war Britain. It confirmed some hard realities that had become apparent in 1947 but were then optimistically forgotten.

- Britain was unable to carry out any major foreign intervention without **the approval of the USA**.
- Britain's 'retreat from empire' would have to continue: from 1956 onwards, military and colonial commitments were scaled down leading to extensive de-colonisation in Africa.
- Britain's economy was unable to carry on alone: in the short term, the Suez affair led to a financial crisis that could only be solved with US assistance; in the longer term, it led to Britain's first application for membership of the **EEC**.

In terms of foreign affairs, the Suez Crisis was thus a significant landmark with important, lasting consequences. The domestic impact of the Suez Crisis was less clear-cut. In the short term, there was a sharp economic crisis, with petrol rationing and a dip in the balance of payments. Politically, Eden was finished. He had ruined his own reputation and the Conservative Party seemed badly, even fatally damaged. The opinion polls swung sharply against the Conservatives and it seemed likely that there would be a divisive struggle within the Party over Eden's successor.

In fact, the Conservative Party recovered remarkably well from the Suez fiasco. Harold Macmillan, having narrowly defeated Butler in the leadership struggle, proved a smooth political operator and rapidly established a high reputation for skilful political management. The economic damage from Suez was also quickly overcome. Although there was a balance of payments crisis in 1958, severe enough to cause

KEY FACT

US approval of British foreign intervention
In 1982, Prime Minister Margaret Thatcher was careful to get US support before sending her task force to the Falklands.

KEY TERM

EEC the European Economic Community 'The Six' was formed by the Messina Conference of 1955 and the Treaty of Rome in 1957. Later, it expanded to take in several additional states, including Britain in 1973. Its name also changed to the EC (European Community) and then the EU (European Union).

the resignation of three Treasury ministers, **Peter Thorneycroft,** Nigel Birch and **Enoch Powell,** the late-1950s was marked by an accelerating consumer boom. Macmillan thus entered the election campaign of 1959 in a strong position. Labour, now led by Hugh Gaitskell, was still suffering from internal feuding and, in particular, from intense disagreement over **Britain's independent nuclear deterrent**.

The result of the 1959 election was another crushing defeat for the Labour Party, whose time in the political wilderness seemed likely to last for years to come. The Suez Crisis had apparently done nothing to damage the Conservatives in the longer term. On the other hand, it may be that the Suez Crisis signalled the emergence of challenging, anti-establishment attitudes in important areas of British society and politics. Opposition to the Suez Crisis, from Labour and the Liberals, among the young and in sections of the national press, was not overwhelming at the time; however, it was a foretaste of what was to come in the Sixties.

HAROLD MACMILLAN IN POWER

Macmillan became prime minister in difficult circumstances. Eden had resigned in disgrace, the Conservatives were down in the opinion polls, and many Conservatives would have preferred Butler as prime minister. Nevertheless, Macmillan proved to be one of the most successful of all Conservative leaders.

Part of Macmillan's success was luck; part of it was the failure of the Labour opposition.

- Economic conditions were moving steadily towards greater personal prosperity; the 1950s was a time of increased car ownership, more and better household goods and greater leisure opportunities.
- Hugh Gaitskell had replaced Clement Attlee as Labour leader in 1955 but he was faced with bitter opposition from the Bevanite Left. The relationship between the leadership and the trade unions was deteriorating badly.

However, part of the explanation was also skill. Macmillan had an elegant style, a mastery of the media, and a good grasp of party politics. He was also very at home in foreign affairs, where he found it easy to outshine Gaitskell. These factors together meant that the Conservative position recovered quickly after Suez; long before the 1959 election, it was obvious that the Conservatives would win.

After the victory of 1959, the political dominance of the Conservatives seemed to be complete.

- Macmillan was widely known as 'Supermac', the name given to him by the cartoonist Vicky.
- The Conservatives could claim once again to be the 'party of economic competence', able to exploit the consumer prosperity of the 1950s and to remind voters that Labour was the party of 'austerity' and devaluations of the pound.
- The Labour Party was almost torn apart in 1960, as Hugh Gaitskell found himself under attack from the Bevanite Left and from the **Campaign for Nuclear Disarmament (CND)**.

WHY DID THE YEARS OF CONSERVATIVE DOMINANCE END IN 1964?

In 1962 and 1963, a series of political developments led to what seemed to be the sudden and surprising end of Conservative dominance. There are at least two different ways of interpreting the fall of the Conservatives.

One view is that the decline of the Conservatives was a combination of short-term 'accidents'.

- Another balance of payments crisis in 1962 prompted Macmillan into a radical reshuffle of his Cabinet – the so-called 'Night of the Long Knives' – in which a third of the government was sacked including the Chancellor, **Selwyn Lloyd**. It is generally agreed by political observers, including Macmillan himself, that this reshuffle was mishandled and did serious damage to both Macmillan and the Conservative Party.
- The last-minute rejection in 1963 of Britain's application to join the EEC was a major setback to Macmillan.
- The Profumo Affair of 1963 was a scandal involving sex, lies and spies in high places; it caused the resignation of the Defence Secretary, **John Profumo**. There was much criticism of Macmillan for being out of touch with

Harold Macmillan as 'Supermac' the name given to him by the cartoonist Vicky.

KEY TERM

Campaign for Nuclear Disarmament the Campaign for Nuclear Disarmament was set up in 1958 and held the annual 'Aldermaston march' every Easter. In 1950, CND played a big role in the Labour Party conference, outvoting Gaitskell and the Labour leadership. But CND declined from this high point and had no influence on the 1964-70 Labour government.

KEY PERSON

Selwyn Lloyd (1904-1978) a Conservative politician who was Foreign Secretary under Eden at the time of Suez; and later Chancellor of the Exchequer under Macmillan. He became famous for 'Stop-Go' economic policies. Although very loyal to Macmillan, he was brutally dismissed in the 'Night of the Long Knives' cabinet reshuffle of 1962.

modern society, especially as it coincided with other scandals such as the **Vassall** spy case and the housing scandal known as '**Rachmanism**'.

- The emergence of **Harold Wilson** as a new youthful and effective leader in succession to Hugh Gaitskell seemingly showed up Macmillan as a relic from an older generation.
- Macmillan was seriously ill following a major operation in 1963 and eventually resigned due to ill-health (although he actually recovered and later regretted his decision to step down).

It might seem that the decline of Conservative dominance and the rise in Labour's fortunes was due to events and personalities, not to any long-term trends. Indeed, the Conservatives recovered from the disasters of 1962–3 and nearly won the 1964 election. Although Macmillan was replaced by the aristocratic and old-fashioned **Sir Alec Douglas-Home**, who seemed an easy opponent for Wilson, the Conservatives were still able to fight a strong campaign and Labour won by only a narrow margin.

Nevertheless, there were significant long-term factors working in Labour's favour in the early 1960s. Sustained prosperity, rising living standards and the Welfare State had created the conditions for a 'social revolution' (see pages 88–93). There was expansion of university education, a new youth culture and the emergence of irreverent, anti-establishment attitudes in the post-Suez generation.

The 1964 election seemed at the time to be a turning point, with the Labour Party more in tune with social trends and likely to replace the Conservatives as the 'natural party of government'. In the event, the high hopes with which Labour came to power were not fulfilled. The real turning point in post-war Britain was not to be 1964, but 1979.

SUMMARY QUESTIONS

1. How successfully did the Labour governments of 1945-51 achieve their aims?

2. What factors enabled the Conservatives to dominate British politics for thirteen years after 1951?

3. Why was Labour able to return to power in 1964?

AS ASSESSMENT: BRITAIN 1929–64

INTRODUCTION

The following assessment exercises provide useful practice for developing your understanding of the historical issues and your examination technique. It is essential to read the questions carefully and to directly answer the specific questions, and not simply to show accurate knowledge. Where possible, you should also look at published mark schemes, or sample answers, to see exactly what the examiner wants. This list of general principles may be useful.

- Take on board the specific instructions of the question, for example, the requirement to use sources and/or your own knowledge.
- Judge the length of your answers precisely in accordance with the marks allocated.
- Write your answers in a direct and accurate form, avoiding vague phrases and excessively long sentences.
- Make sure that your answers are focused on explanation and assessment, not on rigid description.

STUCTURED ESSAY QUESTION IN THE STYLE OF OCR
Study topic:

The impact of the Great Depression on Britain in the 1930s.

(a) Explain how society and the economy in Britain was affected by the impact of the Great Depression in the years 1929–32. [30 marks]

(b) Assess the effects of the economic crisis on the Labour Party in the years 1929–5. [60 marks]

Reading Before answering these questions, you should read the Introduction and Chapters 1 and 2.

How to answer question (a) This answer should be concise and appropriate to a question that should take 10/15 minutes. The answer should explain (not describe) the way various parts of British society were affected by the Depression differentiating between the earlier and later years of the 1930s and between the experiences of different classes and different regions. You should also be prepared to offer an overall interpretation of the 'impact' – whether it was for most people the 'Hungry Thirties' or a decade of affluence.

How to answer question (b) This should be a more substantial essay answer – it carries twice as many marks. The focus of the question is political – on the Labour Party from 1931 to 1935. These key dates are important and your answer should explain both 1931 as turning point in the party's fortunes, and the significance of the 1935 election. A balanced answer would point to the 'trauma' of 1931 as a disaster for the party and a source of lasting bitterness; but would also show appreciation that the party's 'core vote' held up quite well and that after 1935 Labour continued to make modest progress. As with all essay answers, there should be some element of overall interpretation, summing up the overall impact over time.

COURSE ESSAY IN THE STYLE OF AQA
Study topic:

Winston Churchill in opposition and Government 1929–45.

> How successfully did Winston Churchill manage relationships with Britain's wartime allies between 1941 and 1945?   [20 marks]

Reading Before answering this question, you should read the Introduction and Chapter 4. *The People's War* by Angus Calder would provide useful extra reading.

Sample answer

From 1941–5, Winston Churchill was one of the Big Three. Churchill was a key player alongside Roosevelt and Stalin in the Grand Alliance – indeed, Churchill did as much as anyone to bring the Grand Alliance together. It seems obvious that he was enormously successful, keeping Britain at the 'top table' with the two superpowers and gaining great personal prestige in the process. However, Churchill's success was actually very mixed. Although he got most of what he wanted out of Roosevelt at first, Churchill had less and less influence over the USA towards the end of the war. In addition, his relationship with Stalin's Russia was marked by mistakes and failure. The wartime alliance ended in the Cold War and Soviet dominance over Eastern Europe. Churchill had desperately wanted to avoid this but, by 1944, there was no chance of stopping it.

From the time he was made prime minister in the terrible crisis of May 1940, Winston Churchill knew that Britain could never win the war alone. During 1940 and 1941, fighting almost without allies, Britain held out against Hitler's war-machine and refused to surrender or to make a separate peace. However, this could not defeat Hitler, only make the war last long enough for others to win it. Churchill was desperate for allies.

Direct US involvement in the war was out of the question in 1940 because of strong isolationism in Congress. Nevertheless, Churchill established a close and important relationship with President Roosevelt. At first, Roosevelt and his advisers expected Britain to be beaten; it was some time before it became clear that Churchill would consolidate his position as prime minister, defeat the group round Lord Halifax who favoured peace, and carry the country with him in all-out war to the finish. Churchill's personality was very important in 1940, because he made a big impression on US public opinion through US journalists such as the radio reporter Ed Murrow, as well as eventually forging close links with Roosevelt.

The first of these links was the Destroyers for Bases deal, signed in September 1940. This was vital to Britain because the US destroyers were desperately needed for protecting Britain's Atlantic convoys, and also Lend-Lease was a symbol of US support. Once Roosevelt had won the presidential election, he was able to come out into the open and to push the Lend-Lease bill through Congress. Roosevelt drove a hard bargain over Lend-Lease but those who criticise Churchill for giving away too much too easily are wrong: Britain had no other choice. Churchill had actually made everything depend on the USA entering the war before the end of 1941. This gamble came off, partly because of Churchill's skill and persistence in handling Roosevelt, but mostly because Pearl Harbour happened just in time.

Churchill's other major ally, Stalin and the Soviet Union, was gained very suddenly in June 1941 because of Hitler's invasion of the Soviet Union. Churchill was a lifelong anti-communist and his relationship with Stalin was marked by suspicion on both sides. However, the three-way alliance between the Big Three was the only way to win the war. That it was formed at all was Churchill's biggest achievement.

In 1942 and early 1943, while the war was in the balance, the wartime alliance mostly functioned well. Churchill was particularly successful in getting detailed collaboration with the USA, for example, in sharing and using secret intelligence. His personal relationship with Roosevelt got closer and closer and this was reflected in relations between the British side and other key Americans like General Marshall. D-Day in 1944 was one example of how well US–British cooperation generally worked. It is clear that in forming alliances in 1941 and in fighting the war with an effective strategy, Churchill was immensely successful in a way probably nobody else could have been.

Where Churchill failed was in the latter stages of the war, when it became obvious that Hitler and Japan would inevitably be beaten. This was when the emphasis shifted from winning the war to rearranging the post-war world. In this phase, Churchill was mostly a failure, partly because of his own mistakes and partly because, by 1953, Britain was not strong enough to be an equal partner with the two emerging superpowers. Churchill failed to keep a common front with Roosevelt at the Yalta conference in 1945, and he failed either to keep good relations with the USSR or to prevent the Soviet takeover of Poland and most of Eastern and Central Europe. He also failed to face reality over what was going to happen to the British Empire, especially India, after the war.

Despite his faults, Churchill was a great war leader. He had an all-important role at a vital time in 1940–1 and he did more than anyone to make Britain part of the alliance that won the war. In addition, even where he failed, it was less to do with his errors than with the essential weakness of Britain compared to the USA and the USSR.

Examiner's comments

This is an effective and balanced answer. It spends too long on the background in 1940 and it deals better with the early years of the war than with 1943–5. Nevertheless, it has a sound grasp of a range of issues and it offers some differentiated arguments. Overall, it is a Level 4 response.

STRUCTURED SOURCE-BASED QUESTION IN THE STYLE OF AQA
Study topic:

Was there a 'social revolution' in Britain as a result of the Second World War?

Study the following source material and answer the questions which follow.

Source A

Claims that the Second World War 'transformed' the lives of women in Britain are wrong. In reality, attitudes after the war showed remarkable continuity with the 1930s. One historian has claimed that 'women were needed in the factories and the services in 1941–3 and indeed everywhere in the build-up to D-Day in 1944 but then nowhere after 1945'. Official figures show that only 37 per cent of all women were in paid employment in 1951, compared with 34 per cent in 1931. The Second World War had proved to be an exceptional period of little long-term significance. Most women's work had been so tedious that they were pleased to return to 'normal' life. In addition, the post-war legislation of the Attlee government encouraged women to return to the home and breed children.

From *Contemporary Britain* by R. Pearce (1996).

Source B

1 August 1945: I suddenly thought to myself tonight, 'I know why a lot of women have gone into pants. It's a sign they are asserting themselves in some way.' I feel pants are more of a sign of the times than I realised. A growing contempt for man in general creeps over me. For a real craftsman, whether a sweep or a prime minister – hats off. But why this 'Lords of Creation' attitude on men's part? I'm beginning to see that I'm really a clever woman in my own line and not the 'odd' or 'uneducated' woman that I've had dinned into me. I feel that, in the world of tomorrow, marriage will be – will *have* to be – more of a partnership.

From *Nella Last's War: A Mother's Diary 1938–45.* Nella Last was one of many ordinary people encouraged by the Mass Observation Organisation to keep a day-by-day account during the war.

Source C

No one asked us to leave work, and we dared not ask to leave, so in awe were we of the Works. But as the men filtered home there were weddings and homes to set up. There were weddings such as my own where the man had to return back to base afterwards, to finish his service time. We managed to find a house to rent, although in run-down condition, and with my man away. Although I had not been given my cards, I asked for a week off – but I never did go back. I'd had enough, and, in any case, I now had my navy wife's pay-book, which gave me £2.5s.0d a week.

From *D for Doris, V for Victory* by Doris White (1981). In 1945, Doris White was a young woman on war work in Wolverhampton.

(a) Study Source A and use your own knowledge.

Comment on 'post-war legislation' in the context of women in Britain after the Second World War. [3 marks]

(b) Study Source B and use your own knowledge.

How useful is Source B as evidence about the impact of the Second World War upon the lives and attitudes of ordinary women? [7 marks]

(c) Study Sources A, B and C and use your own knowledge.

'During and because of the war, there was a social revolution in Britain; the roles and attitudes of women would never be the same again.'

Explain why you agree or disagree with this statement. [15 marks]

Reading Before answering these questions, you should read the Introduction and Chapter 4. *The People's War* by Angus Calder would provide useful extra reading.

How to answer question (a) This question requires a concise answer, approximately three short sentences aimed to achieve three marks. In general women, especially mothers, were helped by the whole range of welfare state legislation passed between 1946 and 1948, for example, the establishment of the NHS; but the most important specific case was the Family Allowance Act of 1946, which gave money directly to women, not via their husbands.

How to answer question (b) Answers requiring the evaluation of sources should be done with care and precision. It is *not* enough to provide extensive description of the contents of the source, or stereotyped, 'all-purpose' speculation about it. The key issues are:

- What *type* of source is it?
- How far is it well informed?
- For what reasons might it be reliable or otherwise?
- How far is it corroborated by your own knowledge of the topic?

In this case, the source is plainly by an 'ordinary person', not an expert, or a high-level inside witness. The key question is whether Nella Last is *typical* or not of the majority of women in Britain at this time.

How to answer question (c) This should be a more substantial answer, appropriate to the 15 marks allocated. It should include:

- A clear statement of how much and why you agree or disagree
- Sensible explanation using own knowledge
- Precisely selected evidence from the sources
- A brief conclusion restating your point of view.

You might, for example, decide that you disagree and put forward the argument that social change was only temporary and use your own knowledge of documents after the war to prove this. There is useful evidence in Source A and C to support your case. The evidence in Source B can be explained as reflecting an untypical minority of women.

STRUCTURED ESSAY QUESTION IN THE STYLE OF AQA
Study topic:

The extent of economic crisis in Britain after the Second World War and the degree of economic recovery achieved in the years 1947 to 1951.

Read the following source material and answer the questions which follow.

Source A

The year 1947 can be seen in hindsight as a turning point both for the Labour government and for the British economy. From 1948, with the help of Marshall Aid, the economy began to turn the corner from austerity to growth.

From *Austerity and Boom* by C.R. Schenk (1994).

(a) Explain what is meant by 'austerity' in the context of Britain in 1947. [3 marks]

(b) Explain the ways in which Britain faced an economic crisis in 1947. [7 marks]

(c) With what success did Britain achieve economic recovery in the years 1947–51?
[15 marks]

Reading Before answering these questions, you should read Chapters 5 and 6.

How to answer question (a) Your answer should be concise and targeted. It requires three elements –

- a *definition* of the term, with brief examples
- explanation of the *context of 1947*
- a brief *development* of the explanation, perhaps a link to Stafford Cripps.

How to answer question (b) Your answer should explain the 'ways', not describe them. A comprehensive and accurate list would probably be marked at level 2; a developed assessment of the relative importance of two or three key factors would score more highly.

How to answer question (c) You should aim to produce a developed essay answer, appropriate to the marks allocated. An effective, balanced response would deal with:

- an overall assessment of the extent of successful recovery
- the problems faced after 1945, and how the other aims of government (in social policy and foreign affairs) affected the economy

- analysis of any examples of failures and continuing weaknesses
- precisely selected evidence about key aspects of economic recovery
- a brief conclusion summing up your overall case.

STRUCTURED ESSAY QUESTION IN THE STYLE OF OCR
Study topic:
Politics in Britain 1951–1964.

(a) Explain the reasons why the Labour government lost power in 1951.   [30 marks]

(b) Examine the reasons why the Conservatives remained in power throughout the years from 1951–64.   [60 marks]

Reading Before answering these questions, you should read Chapter 6. There is also some useful information to be found in section 1 of the A2 section.

How to answer question (a) This question requires a concise answer that is focused on explanation. Both of the reasons why Labour faced difficulties in the elections of 1950 and 1951 (including the illness and exhaustion of key politicians) should be included as well as the reasons why the Conservatives were bound to do better than 1945 (including the re-organisation of the party under Butler and Lord Woolton). An effective answer would provide a balanced judgment of Labour weaknesses and Conservative strengths.

How to answer question (b) The allocation of marks makes it clear that this should be a much more developed answer than Question (a). To 'examine' the reasons for 13 years of Conservative dominance is not to make a list. A good answer will explain a range of factors and will differentiate between them to show their relative importance. Important factors to be considered include the sustained economic prosperity of the 1950s and the role of key political personalities, both Labour (such as Bevan) and Conservative (perhaps above all Macmillan). It is also vital to provide balanced coverage of the period 1951-64 as a whole.

A2 SECTION: CHAMBERLAIN AND APPEASEMENT, 1937–9

INTRODUCTION: NEVILLE CHAMBERLAIN'S PLACE IN HISTORY

Neville Chamberlain was a talented politician with a distinguished record in domestic politics and government, especially in social reform. However, fairly or unfairly, he is remembered almost solely for his supposed mishandling of the threat of Hitler in the years before the Second World War. In popular myth, Chamberlain is saddled with the image of weakness: the architect of a failed policy of appeasement, from which only the heroic leadership of Winston Churchill could rescue Britain's pride and national greatness. This image reached a peak at the end of the war and in the 1945 election, when memories of the 'ghost of Neville Chamberlain' and the 'Guilty Men' of Munich contributed to Labour's landslide victory. In 2000, celebrations of the sixteenth anniversary of Britain's 'Finest Hour' in 1940 reinforced the Churchil-Chamberlain myths all over again.

Since 1946, when **Keith Feiling** wrote his approving biography, a number of historians have attempted to justify, or at least to provide, a more balanced view of Chamberlain's diplomacy and actions between

KEY TEXT

K. Feiling *The Life of Neville Chamberlain* (1946)

Chamberlain holds aloft the Munich Agreement on his return from Germany, September 1938.

1937 and 1940. In the same period, there has been much critical analysis of Churchill's role and actions during the same wartime period. Nevertheless, Chamberlain's place in history has continued to be dominated by one emotive newsreel image of a man waving a piece of paper at Heston airport, in 1938.

THE WIDER CONTEXT OF APPEASEMENT

In seeking a balanced judgement of Chamberlain's role in the origins of the Second World War, it is important to place his time in office, from 1937–40, in the broader context of appeasement. Chamberlain invented neither the policy of appeasement nor the word. Appeasement can be said to have begun in 1919 with the immediate doubts about the fairness and sustainability of the Treaty of Versailles that emerged almost as soon as it was signed. Even in the vital years from 1937–40 when Chamberlain took such a dominant role in British foreign policy there were many other important factors shaping international affairs.

Understanding Chamberlain's role in the wider context also requires analysis of several key factors outside British politics.

The role of France. France was Britain's major ally. The French had done more than anyone to impose restrictions on Germany in 1919; France was, supposedly, the major military power in Europe. Blocking Hitler's aggression was thus above all a French responsibility. By the 1930s, however, leadership and morale of the French army was in a bad state. French politics was riddled with divisions and defeatism. In March 1936, France took a passive, non-interventious approach to the Spanish civil war. Thus one key reason why Chamberlain took such a leading role in appeasement from 1937 was that the French governments were more than willing to let him do so. The big question is whether Chamberlain was realistic and correct in his view of French weakness; would a different policy from Britain have stiffened French resolve?

The problem of Stalin and the USSR. The Soviet Union was treated as almost an outlaw state in the interwar period: it was not involved in the post-war peace settlement and was regarded with fear and suspicion by the rest of Europe. These fears were intensified in the vital years 1936–8 by **Stalin's purges** and by Soviet involvement in the Spanish Civil War. Any attempt to use the Soviet Union as a counter force against Hitler was hugely difficult for the western democracies – yet it was almost impossible to protect the successor states of East Central Europe any other way. Chamberlain was notably anti-communist and has been attacked for failing to exploit the opportunities for allying with the Soviet Union– but such an alliance may have been practically impossible. Much depends on

KEY THEME

Little Democracies refers to the new states formed in 1919–20, such as Poland, Hungary and Czechoslovakia.

KEY TREATY

The Locarno Treaties (1925) were an attempt to get a voluntary agreement from Germany to accept the post-war territorial settlement. At the time there was much international optimism, sometimes known as the 'Locarno honeymoon'.

the judgement of Stalin, was he an 'abnormal' dictator with whom no rational agreements could ever have been made in peacetime?

The problem of the Successor States. In the 1919-20 peace treaties, the **Little Democracies** were formed. States like Czechoslovakia and Poland were small and vulnerable, dependent upon protection against the revival of German and Russian power. By the 1930s, it was clear that such protection would not come from the League of Nations, or from the isolationist USA. The charge against Chamberlain is that he was guilty of 'selling out' the Czechs in 1938 - the key question is whether there was ever a way of protecting the 'Little Democracies', other than by an alliance with Stalin.

The problem of the Great Depression. The consequences of the Wall Street Crash and the onset of the Great Depression were significant in foreign affairs. The depression had much to do with Hitler's coming to power. It blew away international economic cooperation and the optimism of the Locarno honeymoon. It distracted and unsettled the governments of the western democracies; and slowed down their efforts to rearm.

The problem of Hitler. The basis of Chamberlain's appeasement policy was that the right way of dealing with Germany was to accept Hitler as an international statesman with legitimate grievancies. Critics such as Churchill and Ernest Bevin argued from an early stage that Hitler was an aggressive dictator who could only be blocked by force. The key question is how Hitler would have responded to a firm line from the Western powers? Would he have been stopped (or even overthrown by internal opposition in Germany) if Britain and France had threatened war over Czechoslovakia in 1938? If so, Chamberlain's policy was disastarous; but if not, if the cause of war was Hitler, then Chamberlain cannot be blamed too much.

THE ORIGINS OF APPEASEMENT BEFORE 1937

Appeasement existed long before Chamberlain reached Downing Street. In 1919, Lloyd George said of Versailles: 'we will have to do it all over again in 25 years at three times the cost'. The British economic expert J.M. Keynes was influential in promoting a more conciliatory policy towards Germany, in order to avoid disastrous economic consequences for Europe if Germany collapsed. Even French policy towards Germany changed, the **Locarno Treaties** of 1925 were based on co-operation with Germany, not coercion. The terrible losses of the Great War strengthened ideas of pacifism, disarmament and international agreements. Appeasement was fostered by a belief in collective security and the League of Nations. Appeasement also seemed to be a realistic policy because of the American withdrawal into isolationism.

From 1933, the latent 'German question' became the actual Hitler threat. Hitler began to rearm; German propaganda promised to tear up Versailles. At this time, Hitler's threats were mostly bluff. It was only in November 1937, at the Hossbach conference, that he told his military chiefs of his real plans for war.

Until 1937, the prime responsibility for responding to the German threat was French. France after all had signed treaties with several of the Successor States. In 1935, France had made a pact with the Soviet Union to protect Czechoslovakia against aggression. France had a common border with Germany and could rely on, supposedly, the best army in Europe.

French policy, however, was passive. The left-wing Popular Front government tended towards pacifism; the right-wing government that replaced it preferred the idea of an alliance with Mussolini's Italy. In Britain, the National Government headed by Stanley Baldwin was preoccupied with the economic problems of the Great Depression. Baldwin was a natural conciliator, determined to avoid war. He had also been impressed by Nazi propaganda about the all-powerful Luftwaffe and overrated the threat of destruction by bombing. In 1935-36, Baldwin's government took a soft approach to Mussolini's invasion of Abyssinia; very few British politicians wanted to confront the fascist dictators.

When Chamberlain became prime minister in May 1937, therefore, the policy of appeasement was already deeply rooted. It is important not to exaggerate Chamberlain's importance, or his ability to control events. Many British historians and commentators have made Chamberlain and British foreign policy all-important when, in reality, Chamberlain was merely one of many key players in the events that led Europe into war.

Timeline of appeasement

The basic story of appeasement is dealt with in AS section, page 25–29. The following timescale provides a summary.

1919–33: the roots of appeasement.	Growing doubts about the permanence of the Versailles Treaty; the isolationist foreign policy of the USA and the Soviet Union; Stresemann and the Locarno Treaties; preoccupation with the economic impact of the Great Depression.
1933–7: the threat of Hitler.	Hitler's rise to power and German re-armament; Mussolini and Abyssinia, 1935; the Rhineland reoccupation of

KEY EVENT

The Hossbach Conference was a secret meeting in November 1937 at which Hitler informed his top military commanders of his plans for an aggressive war.

1937–9: high tide of appeasement.

1939–40: the end of appeasement?

1936; the Spanish Civil War and the policy of non-intervention; the role of Stanley Baldwin.

Chamberlain's appointment as prime minister May 1937; Hitler's **Hossbach Conference** November 1937; the *Anschluss* March 1938; the Munich Conference September 1938; Hitler's occupation of Prague in March 1939.

Failed attempts to ally with the USSR in blocking Hitler; the Nazi–Soviet Pact August 1939; Hitler's conquest of Poland in September 1939; the 'Phoney War'; prospects of making peace after the fall of France in May 1940; the consolidation of Churchill's position and the commitment to total war.

CHAMBERLAIN AND FOREIGN POLICY 1937–40

From 1937 to the Munich Conference

Chamberlain inherited appeasement to which he added the stamp of his own personality: he took the lead, with the French content to follow. Chamberlain was often obstinately self-confident. It is at least partly justified, therefore, to see British foreign policy between 1937 and 1939 as something of a one-man show. The key events of 1938, for example, were the meetings at Berchtesgaden, Bad Godesberg and Munich, where Chamberlain put such emphasis on personal diplomacy. After the resignation of Anthony Eden in 1938, the key British policymakers, such as the Ambassador in Berlin, Nevile Henderson, Alexander Cadogan at the Foreign Office, and Chamberlain's special representative Sir Horace Wilson, were all supportive of Chamberlain's line.

Chamberlain's policies were based on fixed principles.

- He was genuinely horrified by the prospect of another European war and saw himself as a peacemaker.
- He was genuinely committed to social reform, which would be prevented by an inevitably expensive war.
- He was convinced that Britain was not militarily ready for war in 1937 or 1938.

- He believed that Germany had valid grievances that should be rectified.
- He assumed that British public opinion was united in supporting him.

In 1937 and 1938, Chamberlain was convinced that it was possible and desirable to reach an agreement with Germany and Italy. In the early months of 1938 leading up to the *Anschluss*, Chamberlain had increasing disagreements with his talented and popular Foreign Minister, Anthony Eden. When these disagreements came to a head, Eden resigned. The new Foreign Secretary, Lord Halifax, supported appeasement and was in the House of Lords leading Chamberlain to handle the House of Commons. In 1938 there was also a change of government in France. The new **Daladier** government, with Georges Bonnet as Foreign Minister, was much more disposed to appeasement.

1938–9: From Munich to Prague

Chamberlain was also a powerful prime minister, with a good control of Parliament and the Cabinet. He could face down what opposition there was from the Labour Party relatively easily, as well as that from Winston Churchill and his **Focus group**. This is why Munich appears as such a personal triumph for Chamberlain: he could claim that it was *his* policy and that it had been successful. He had faced up to Hitler in their September meetings: Hitler had been pushed into a conference he did not want and had negotiated like a reasonable statesman.

Ultimately, the main agreement of appeasement was short-lived: it lasted only until March 1939 and Hitler's occupation of Prague. Now Munich seemed useless. Hitler had become stronger and more dangerous than ever and Stalin had decided after Munich that cooperating with the western democracies was not a viable way of protecting the Soviet Union.

There were three great questions in 1938 and 1939.

- Why did Chamberlain persist with appeasement after Hitler's occupation of Prague in March 1939?
- How effectively did the government use the breathing space gained by Munich to push through rearmament?
- Why, once it became clear that Hitler's next move would be against Poland, did Britain not make an anti-Hitler alliance with the Soviet Union?

1939-40: From Prague to the fall of France

Chamberlain sincerely changed his policy in March 1939. He felt Hitler had cheated him and must be resisted. He gave guarantees to Poland; an Anglo-French military mission was sent to Moscow to discuss possible

KEY THEME

Chamberlain and Eden Many historians consider Eden's resignation to have been welcome to Chamberlain, if not engineered by him. After Eden was gone, Chamberlain took personal control of foreign policy.

KEY PERSON

Daladier (1884-1970) Prime Minister of France at the time of Munich in 1938. Daladier was generally content to take a back seat and to allow Chamberlain to make the running in negotiating with Hitler.

KEY TERM

Focus group was the circle of advisers and colleagues who supported Churchill in his political activities while he was politically isolated in the 1930s.

joint measures to protect Poland and British rearmament was stepped up, especially aircraft production. In September 1939, however, Chamberlain reluctantly declared war. He kept to the belief that the only realistic outcome was some king of negotiated settlement. Most influential Conservatives, including Lord Halifax, agreed with him. The result, after the rapid German victory in Poland, was the 'Phoney War'. Britain and France took no military initiatives but waited for Hitler's next move. When it came, in May 1940, Chamberlain proved an ineffective war leader. He was forced to resign in humiliating circumstances. His sternest critic before the war, Winston Churchill, replaced him as prime minister. Only when Churchill consolidated his position and rallied the government and the nation behind him, did appeasement really end, and the war really begin.

The case against Chamberlain

On the surface, Chamberlain's ultimate failure is beyond dispute. He misread Hitler's intentions. The war he tried so hard to avoid began in September 1939. He resigned in disgrace with the war going badly in May 1940. Churchill's success in became the hero of Britain's 'Finest Hour' seemed to prove the futility of all Chamberlain's policies. Here are the main charges against him:

- he was guilty of concealment and manipulation, deceiving public opinion
- he was obsessed with his own authority and jealous of 'stars' like Eden
- he overrated his skills of personal diplomacy and was taken in by Hitler
- he persisted too long with appeasement after it had visibly failed
- his government did not rearm urgently enough
- he refused to try to reach an effective alliance with the Soviet Union
- he was too ready to force the Czechs to surrender to German demands
- he undermined the chances of firm action by France
- after September 1939, he failed either to fight the war effectively or to have any realistic plan to end it by diplomacy.

The case for the defence

Many of the criticisms of Chamberlain were unfair, even simplistic. Appeasement was, in itself, an honorable policy. The myth that Chamberlain was absolutely wrong about everything, and that Churchill was absolutely right, perhaps has some validity for 1940 but simply does not fit the facts of 1938-39. Here are the arguments in defence of his policy and actions:

- his policy was backed by the mass of British political and public opinion
- treating Hitler like a reasonable statesman was a justified policy in 1938
- Britain could not fight a war simultaneously in the Far East, the Mediterranean and Europe
- his analysis of French military weakness was correct; and Chamberlain was supported in his cautious policies by his top military advisers
- between 1938 and 1940, Britain made just enough advances in fighter aircraft and development of radar to be able to survive the war
- many of his opponents, including Churchill were wrong – the policies they recommended would have led to defeat and disaster
- Britain's military and naval resources were over-stretched, war would undermine the gradual economic recovery of the late 1930s
- being seen to try every diplomatic means to avert war was vital to keeping the support of the Empire when Britain finally went to war.

CONCLUSION

Chamberlain's place in history has been shaped by what happened after he resigned as prime minister in 1940. Churchill, by a very narrow margin, convinced the war cabinet to fight on. By an even narrower margin, Britain avoided being defeated by Germany until the nation was saved by alliances with the USSR and with the Americans in 1941. Chamberlain retired from politics, already a dying man, in October 1940. Already then, and ever afterwards, he was in Churchill's shadow. On the other hand, Chamberlain was extremely loyal to Churchill's new government in 1940. Churchill himself was very considerate towards Chamberlain after his fall from power; Chamberlain repaid this by doing nothing to undermine Churchill during the tense weeks when he was consolidating his wartime government. A balanced judgement of Chamberlain and appeasement may well conclude that he was a failure, but an honourable one and that both his mistakes and his relative importance for the wider causes of the Second World War have been too often overstated.

ASSESSING CHAMBERLAIN AND APPEASEMENT

The key to assessing the validity of various interpretations of this complex topic is to develop a clear independent interpretation of your own. Sources cannot be evaluated by any external, second-hand rules. Below is a selection of material from a variety of perspectives, both from modern historians and from key contemporaries. From the standpoint of your own interpretation, make a critical assessment of the usefulness, sufficiency and reliability of each source. It will be difficult, but it will make life in examinations a lot easier!

A2 ASSESSMENT: CHAMBERLAIN AND APPEASEMENT, 1937–9

Source-based question in the style of OCR

STUDY TOPIC: CHAMBERLAIN AND APPEASEMENT, 1937–9

Source A

Chamberlain returned to Britain triumphant. He received a hero's welcome from a nation hugely relieved that there was not going to be a war after all. He was particularly pleased with himself because he had got Hitler to sign a declaration that the Munich Agreement and the Anglo–German Naval Treaty were 'symbols of the desire of our two peoples never to go to war with one another again'. This was, for Chamberlain, his 'peace with honour'. For Hitler, it was a piece of paper of no significance.

M. Roberts, *Britain 1946–64: The Challenge of Change* (2001).

Source B

Although appeasement failed when it was confronted by the aggressive, irresponsible behaviour of Nazi Germany, it was never a misguided policy. The normal basis of appeasement is the assumption that agreement is possible. For as long as this assumption holds good, appeasement is the necessary policy, combining expediency with morality. Only when all the evidence finally showed that Hitler's nature made appeasement impracticable, was it right to abandon the policy.

M. Gilbert, *The Roots of Appeasement* (1966).

Source C

There is no doubt that the Chamberlain government did consciously set out to control and manipulate the press in those years. The most obvious consequence was that no realistic alternative policy to appeasement could ever be consistently articulated in the British press, nor were facts and figures that might have supported such an alternative policy ever put in front of the majority of the British public. Thus, Chamberlain successfully obscured the divisions over his policy that existed not only in Westminster but also throughout the country. Public opinion polls were in their infancy in the late 1939s, but even a glance at the polls which were taken shows that, in its support for Chamberlain and appeasement, the press was dangerously out of step with public opinion. One poll in February 1938 asked:

'Do you approve of Mr Chamberlain's foreign policy?' The answers were: *Yes*: 26 per cent; *No*: 58 per cent; *No opinion*: 16 per cent.

R. Cockett, *Twilight of Truth: Chamberlain, Appeasement and the Manipulation of the Press* (1989).

Source D

In 1938, unlike Churchill, Chamberlain had knowledge of what passed for the French war plan, and of the latest report from the British Chiefs of Staff. The French plan was to wait behind the Maginot Line until the British had expanded their army and economic blockade had begun to bite on Germany. This was not a strategy that would bring speedy relief to the Czechs (as the Poles were to find out a year later). The Chiefs were adamant that there was nothing that Britain or France could do to prevent Germany from inflicting a decisive defeat on Czechoslovakia. Britain was still a year away from the time when its rearmament programme would be substantially complete.

J. Charmley, *Chamberlain and the Lost Peace* (1989).

1 (a) Explain which of Sources A and C provides the more convincing historical judgement of British public opinion towards the policy of appeasement in 1938.
[15 marks]

   (b) Using Sources A–D, explain why Chamberlain's actions and motives in 1938–9 have caused disagreement between historians. [30 marks]

2 Explain why Britain did not enter into an alliance with the Soviet Union in 1939 in order to block the threat from Hitler's Germany. [45 marks]

Reading Before answering these questions, you should read Section 1. There is also some useful material in the AS section, Chapter 3. *The Origins of the Second World War in Europe* by P. M. H. Bell (1997) provides an excellent overview.

How to answer question 1 (a) This answer needs to be concise, in accordance with the marks allocated. It requires a *relative* assessment therefore it is essential to make your mind up about which of the two sources is the more convincing *before* commencing to write. This means balancing the strengths and weaknesses of each source against the other. Remember, too, that your answer cannot be second-hand – it is essential to know clearly what your own interpretation is before trying to assess someone else's.

How to answer question 1 (b) This question requires a balanced overview. Before looking at Sources A-D, you will need to sum up the issues in the light of your own knowledge, almost certainly bringing into play some of the other historians you are familiar with, then Sources A-D can be used selectively to exemplify the issues. To start out by describing the contents of Sources A-D would *not* be a good beginning!

How to answer question 2 This question requires a developed essay answer. You will need a clearly differentiated argument to explain a range of reasons and their relative importance. You will also need a good grasp of the essential issues.

- When did the threat from Hitler's Germany become urgent?
- How might an alliance with the USSR have been helpful in blocking this?
- Why would such an alliance have been difficult to achieve?
- What were the key reasons why there was no alliance?

You need to consider a wide range of factors beyond the British and Soviet policy makers such as long-term factors going back to 1917, public and political opinion in Britain, the attitude of Poland and so on.

A2 SECTION: BRITISH POLITICS AND SOCIETY, 1951–97

INTRODUCTION

1951 was a landmark in British politics. It marked the end of 'austerity' and the beginnings of the post-war boom. It marked the end of the first Labour government having real political power and a working majority. It marked the beginning of a period during which the Conservatives would be in power for 35 years out of 46.

The legacy of the Attlee governments

What was the 'Attlee Legacy' in 1951? The Attlee government had achieved much of what they set out to do. Between 1947 and 1951, there was a considerable degree of economic recovery from the severe crisis of 1945–7. Key industries had been nationalised and the Welfare State was created. There was full employment. Ernest Bevin's work as Foreign Secretary had ensured continuation of the 'special relationship' with the USA and the formation of **NATO**. Yet after losing power in 1951, Labour experienced only two frustrating periods in office until the Blair landslide in 1997. The history of British politics and society between 1951 and 1997 is framed by the end of Attlee's government and the beginning of Blair's.

TRENDS AND DEVELOPMENTS, 1951–97
Economy and society

The years 1951–73 saw a sustained period of full employment and relative prosperity – the long post-war boom. Between 1973 and 1979, there followed a period of intense economic difficulties, beginning with the **oil price crisis**. 1979–90 witnessed the period of 'Thatcherism', with a swing towards 'market values', considerable industrial unrest and privatisation of nationalised concerns. Throughout the post-war years, there was extensive social and cultural change, with the emergence of a youth culture, the advance of women, vast developments in the mass media and the growth of multiculturalism. The Britain of 1997 was radically different from the Britain of 1951.

KEY TERM

NATO The North Atlantic Treaty Organisation formed in 1949. One comment about NATO was that 'it was to keep the Russians out; the Americans in; and the Germans down'.

KEY EVENT

Oil price crisis In 1973, the newly formed OPEC (Organisation of Petroleum Producing and Exporting Countries) took action to raise the international price of oil supplies. This led to a fuel crisis in Britain and many western countries that helped to bring about several years of economic recession.

KEY TERM

SDP (Social Democratic Party) was formed in 1981 by the 'Gang of Four'– the moderate Labour politicians, Roy Jenkins, Shirley Williams, David Owen and Bill Rodgers. This breakaway was in reaction to the dominance of the Labour Party by the extreme Left after 1979. Later, the SDP formed an electoral alliance with the Liberals, which eventually led to a merger in 1988.

Politics and government

The years 1951–1964 were marked by the dominance of moderate Conservative governments under Churchill, Eden and Macmillan. Between 1964 and 1979, there was a period of mostly Labour governments under Wilson and Callaghan, interrupted by the Conservative government under Edward Heath of 1970–4. 1979–1997 was the era of 'Thatcherite' Conservatism: first the domination of Mrs Thatcher through three successive election victories, then the subsequent period when the Conservative government under John Major attempted to adjust to the consequences of Thatcher's fall. During those years, the Labour Party fell into decline as it faced internal divisions and the formation of the breakaway **SDP**, and became virtually unelectable as shown by the catastrophic defeat in 1983 and 1987. Thereafter, the Labour Party experienced a revival under Neil Kinnock, John Smith and finally Tony Blair.

From 1969–1998, there was constant political preoccupation with the problems of security in Northern Ireland.

Foreign affairs

The period was marked by a slow and uneven 'retreat from empire', with further decolonisation and gradual acceptance of Britain's reduced world role. The continuance of the Cold War enhanced Britain's 'special relationship' with the USA, while Britain's relationship to Europe grew more complex. Britain did not join the EEC until 1973; even after British entry, the precise nature of Britain's role in Europe remained contentious.

Key themes

Out of these issues and themes, several key questions arise.

- How far was there really a post-war consensus?
- Was there continuous economic decline?
- Did the social and cultural changes amount to a social revolution?
- Did Thatcherism fundamentally change the direction of British politics?
- Why was the Labour Party unsuccessful for so much of this period and yet able to win power so spectacularly in 1997?
- Why was Europe such a difficult issue for British governments and people?
- Why were the problems of Northern Ireland so difficult to overcome?

SECTION 1

To what extent was there a post-war consensus between 1951 and 1979?

INTRODUCTION

At the general election of 1951, the business of government passed from Labour into Conservative hands. What was noticeable, once the electoral froth had subsided, was how little had actually changed. Attlee's patriotic socialists gave way to Churchill's social patriots but there was to be no attempt to redefine the relationship between government and people that had been established by Labour in the immediate post-war years. The incoming Conservative government inherited a welfare state underpinned by a mixed economy, along with a continuing commitment to full employment.

Dilwyn Porter *Never-Never land: Britain under the Conservatives 1951–64* in from *Blitz to Blair* ed. N. Tiratsoo, 1997.

Dilwyn Porter's claim sets out one of the central ideas about post-war Britain – that of a 'post-war consensus': that the sense of national unity, which developed during and because of the 'People's War', was continued and consolidated by the Attlee legacy. Many historians agree with Porter's view of the essential continuity of British society and politics from 1951, many would also consider that this so-called post-war consensus remained in effect until the end of the post-war boom in the 1970s and the turning point of Margaret Thatcher's election victory in 1979.

The legacy of the war years

In one important respect, there was indeed a post-war consensus after the Second World War. Politicians on both sides had been moulded by the war. Attlee, Churchill and Eden had all worked together in the wartime coalition. Macmillan had had important responsibilities liaising with the army. **Roy Jenkins** was a code breaker at Bletchley Park. **Edward Heath** and **Denis Healey** served in the army. **Jim Callaghan** was proud of his navy record. Prime ministers until Wilson in 1964 had fought in the First World War, too. In all political parties, the shared experiences of war led to a broadly similar view of the post-war world.

It is also true that the public knockabout of Britain's two-party system has often exaggerated the differences between politicians and parties and has hidden the fact that ministers in all the parties tended to have very similar backgrounds – usually an independent or grammar school

KEY PEOPLE

Roy Jenkins (1920-2002) was a leading minister in the Wilson government of 1964-70, first as Home Secretary then as Chancellor. Strongly pro-Europe, he became President of the EEC Commission in 1977. He was one of the founders of the SDP in 1981.

Edward Heath (1916-) was Macmillan's chief negotiator for the application to join the EEC in 1961. He became leader of the Conservatives in 1965, and prime minister after the 1970 election. His great success was in securing membership of the EU in 1973; but his time in office coincided with the recession after the 1973 oil-price crisis. He was narrowly defeated in the two general elections of 1974 and replaced by Mrs Thatcher as Tory leader in 1975.

education followed by a degree from Oxford or Cambridge University. Tony Blair's background would have fitted the Conservative mould as well or better than Edward Heath's would. Nevertheless, the unifying effect of the Second World War had an especially strong influence after 1945. In post-war British politics, and in the popular culture of cinema and television, the Second World War was not so much part of history as an all-pervasive state of mind.

There is less agreement about whether this consensus was a good thing. Throughout the post-war years, many outside observers in Europe and the USA expressed deep concern about Britain's obsession with the past, with the war and with the empire. Economic historians (see Section 4, pages 104–112) have disagreed sharply about the degree to which the period from 1951–1979 was a time of economic failure and wasted opportunities. Right-wing Conservatives argued that the continuation of the Attlee legacy was a tragic 'socialist' mistake, burdening Britain with excessive social spending and inefficient state control of industry. Left-wing Bevanites argued that the Attlee legacy was not nearly socialist enough, having missed a glorious opportunity to break down the dominance of British society by the 'establishment'.

Political tensions

Indeed, resolving the debates about the direction of Britain in the post-war years requires analysis of the tensions within the two main political parties. The Labour Party was subject to a series of intense internal divisions and personality clashes throughout its post-war history. Moreover, in one important respect, the post-war Labour Party did *not* move in tune with the idea of the post-war consensus: Labour did not become a social democratic party. In West Germany, 1959 was a key turning point when the socialist SPD radically reformed itself, dropping its traditional Marxist ideology in favour of modernisation and social democracy. 1959, after a third successive election defeat, would have provided an ideal moment for the Labour Party to do the same; the post-war consensus would have been much stronger if they had. However, this did not happen. Not until the 1990s did Labour finally drop **Clause 4** and other symbols of the Left in favour of Blair's Third Way (see page 127).

The Conservative Party, having been generally successful in maintaining party unity (and thus generally successful in retaining political power), was overtaken in its turn by internal ideological rifts from the 1970s. Margaret Thatcher's successful rebellion against Edward Heath in 1975 probably marked the point at which the Conservative Party shifted away from the post-war consensus. Thatcher's election successes at first masked the degree of party divisions, but these splits continued to exist and were brought out in the open after her fall in 1990.

Making judgements about the post-war consensus, therefore, is difficult. It involves analysis of the political parties, of economics, and of the issues of foreign policy. It also involves subjective interpretations of key personalities.

- Does Attlee, for example, deserve to be remembered as the greatest of Labour prime ministers?
- Was Harold Macmillan really 'Supermac', or a superficial failure?
- Was Harold Wilson a master tactician holding the Labour Party together against impossible odds, or the leader who had the best chance to establish a strong modernising Labour government but wasted it?
- Was Edward Heath the last defender of 'One Nation' Conservatism before the party swung violently to the Right under Thatcher?
- Was Margaret Thatcher a necessary and long overdue saviour, wrestling both the Conservative Party and the country from the wrong direction followed since 1945?

HOW FAR WAS THE ATTLEE LEGACY CONTINUED BY THE CONSERVATIVE GOVERNMENTS OF 1951–64?
Politics

The Conservative Party of the 1950s could hardly be described as right wing. Neither Churchill nor Eden made any radical moves to alter relationships between the government and the trade unions. Although the steel industry was denationalised in 1953, there was no systematic attempt to reverse what Labour had done between 1945 and 1951. In addition, Harold Macmillan's government did far more to consolidate the post-war consensus than to challenge it. According to the journalist James Margach, who knew him as an MP in the industrial North East during the Depression, Macmillan was 'one of the two most left-wing post-war prime ministers' (Margach's other choice was Attlee).

On election night in 1959, Labour's third successive election defeat, the pro-Labour historian Alan Bullock was interviewed on BBC television. He expressed the fear that there would be a swing to the Right in British politics and that the steady move towards greater equality in Britain since 1940 might be reversed. These fears were not justified – at least not at the time. The trend Bullock was predicting did not come about until the late 1970s. After 1959, Macmillan's government continued to follow very centrist policies; for example, the expansion of higher education and the first moves toward comprehensive schools in the early 1960s.

KEY TERM

Clause 4 was the commitment in the Labour Party constitution to maintain state control of nationalized industries. By the 1980s, it was seen as out-of-date and a grave electoral handicap. 'New Labour' abandoned Clause 4 in 1994.

Economic policy

The continuation of the post-war consensus under the Conservative government was referred to as 'Butskellism'. This term is often overused but its very existence is revealing. R.A. Butler had been the architect of the 1944 Education Act. He was a key figure in the Conservative Party, Chancellor of Exchequer, 1951–55 and a serious contender for the leadership in 1957 and again in 1963. Hugh Gaitskell became leader of the Labour Party after Attlee and was very much from the Right of the Labour Party. As Chancellor, he had clashed with Nye Bevan and the Labour Left in 1951 over the costs of the NHS.

After the 1959 election, Gaitskell became bogged down in increasingly open feuds with the left-wingers in his own party, especially over nuclear disarmament. One of the key features in 'Butskellism' was the idea that Butler and Gaitskell had much more in common with each other than with the rival wings of their own parties. Moreover, it was not simply a matter of these two individuals. Macmillan and Heath for the Conservatives, along with **Anthony Crosland** and Roy Jenkins on the Labour side, easily fitted into the Butskellite specification.

Foreign policy

Foreign affairs were a significant element of the Attlee legacy and the post-war consensus, which has been summed up as 'a commitment to maintain both the Welfare State and national greatness'. One of the most contentious issues for the Labour Left throughout the post-war period was their dissatisfaction with a Labour leadership that held firmly to the US alliance, to large-scale defence commitments, including the independent nuclear deterrent, and to the anti-Soviet policies of the Cold War.

Such policies were very important to the Attlee government after 1945. Men like Attlee himself, Ernest Bevin and Hugh Dalton had been moulded by their experience in Churchill's wartime coalition. More than that, Labour politicians were acutely sensitive to the old claims that 'socialism' was unpatriotic and unreliable; they were anxious to prove the opposite. Ernest Bevin was a veteran of long and bitter battles with left-wingers and communists during the Thirties. He was a sincere admirer of Churchill and a natural 'Cold Warrior', proud of his success in the formation of NATO and in keeping the 'special relationship' in good repair. Although many on the Labour Left were unhappy with such policies, they were never able to overturn them. Therefore, there was little in the foreign sphere that the Conservative Party felt the need to alter after 1951.

The post-war consensus in foreign affairs was not total. It was placed under severe strain by Eden's Suez fiasco, which led to sharp attacks on

> **KEY PERSON**
>
> **Anthony Crosland** (1918-1977) Crosland was a key Labour theorist, famous for writings such as *The Future of Socialism* in 1956. He promoted ideas of economic efficiency and was often attacked by the Labour left. He was Foreign Secretary in Callaghan's government when he died in 1977.

Eden from the Labour side (see page 53–55). However, the point about the Suez Crisis is that it did not lead to lasting differences between the parties precisely because the Conservative Party virtually renounced it. Even at the time a key minister, **Anthony Nutting**, resigned in protest; the Tory Chief Whip, Edward Heath, was unofficially in agreement with the anti-Eden sentiment in his own party and with most Labour critics.

From 1957, Harold Macmillan (who had been a leading hawk in favour of the Suez intervention) read the lessons of the affair and was quick to mend fences with the USA and to reassess the direction of British policy. By 1960, Macmillan was making his **'Wind of Change' speech**, opening the way for rapid decolonisation across Africa. This, of course, was a policy with which most Labour MPs totally supported.

The other conclusion Macmillan reached after Suez was the necessity of British entry to the European Economic Community (EEC). Had the 1961 British application for entry succeeded, it might well have put the post-war consensus under pressure; at that time, the bulk of the Labour Party was, for a variety of reasons both on the Left and on the Right, opposed to British involvement in Europe (see pages 97–98). However, de Gaulle's veto in 1963 prevented the issue from being put to the test.

It is significant that when Labour came to power under Harold Wilson's government, it went through with Britain's second application for entry to the EEC in 1967. It has been claimed that Wilson did this knowing that it would fail (and that Wilson actually *wanted* it to fail), but, even so, Wilson's 1967 application provided convincing evidence that the post-war consensus was still essentially in being. Foreign affairs remained an area in which differences between the two main parties were insignificant compared with the **bitter divisions in the Labour movement** itself.

The significance of the 1964 general election

Those historians who have argued the case for a post-war consensus between 1951 and 1979 inevitably play down the significance of Labour's election victory in 1964. Yet it seemed an important turning point at the time (see page 56): the end of what critics called 'thirteen years of Tory misrule', symbolised by the replacement of the aristocratic Alec Douglas-Home with Harold Wilson. The Labour campaign made much of the theme of modernisation; Wilson was fond of talking about the 'white heat of the technological revolution'. There was certainly a public mood of expectancy in 1964 (and again in 1966) that reflected the sense that 1960s Britain was going through fundamental social and cultural change.

On the other hand, there was no real change of political direction. Firstly, 1964 did not see the Labour governments under Wilson and Callaghan

KEY PERSON

Anthony Nutting (1920-1999) was a minister in the Eden government and a specialist on colonial affairs. In 1956, he resigned in protest against the Suez invasion.

KEY EVENT

'Wind of Change' speech was made by Harold Macmillan in Capetown in 1960. It set the tone for Britain's future policy of decolonisation in Africa.

KEY THEME

Bitter divisions in the Labour movement Labour had internal divisions in the 1950s and early 1960s. Hugh Gaitskell was under constant attack from the Bevanite Left and the trade unions. The 1960 party conference was especially divisive, Gaitskell was outvoted on the issue of nuclear weapons.

succeed in carrying through the radical promises of 1964. Secondly, their policies were not so different from what the Conservatives would have done and the emphasis on economic modernisation, for example, was just as strong under Edward Heath after 1970 as it was under Wilson from 1964–70.

WHY WERE THE LABOUR GOVERNMENTS BETWEEN 1964 AND 1979 UNABLE TO ACHIEVE MORE SUCCESS?

When Harold Wilson came to power in 1964, optimism among Labour supporters was high. Wilson himself appeared to be a talented leader with wide support in the country. It seemed that Labour was far more modern than the Conservatives, far more in tune with the rapid social and cultural changes of the 1960s. Although Labour had only a small majority in 1964, the 1966 election strengthened Labour's position. Wilson himself suggested that Labour had replaced the Tories as 'the natural party of government' and was ready to 'break the mould of British politics'.

During the next fifteen years, these high hopes resulted in disappointment and disillusionment. Wilson's government ran into economic difficulties and the devaluation of the pound in 1967 was a bitter blow, apparently confirming Conservative claims that Labour governments invariably led to devaluation, as had happened in 1931 and 1947. Despite Wilson's legendary tactical skills, internal divisions plagued the party and these were eventually to run out of control during the 1970s.

Wilson achieved far less as prime minister than might have been expected of someone with his great talents and given the favourable situation he inherited in 1964. Labour was surprisingly defeated in the 1970 general election and Wilson suddenly resigned early in his second term of office, in 1976. By 1978–9, Jim Callaghan was facing the 'Winter of Discontent' (unofficial strikes from the trade union movement) and the virtual paralysis of his government (see page 86–87). Labour did not simply lose power in 1979: it went into a political wilderness that was worse, and lasted much longer, than the disasters that had hit Labour after 1931.

Political developments, 1964–79.

1964	Labour in power with only a small majority.
1966	Convincing Labour victory over Heath and the Conservatives.
1967	Economic crisis and devaluation of sterling.
1969	Withdrawal of 'In Place of Strife'; abandonment of trade union reform.
1970	Surprise Conservative election victory.

1973	British entry to the EEC; OPEC oil price crisis and miners' strike.
1974	General election (February) with inconclusive outcome but leads to Wilson's third government.
	General election (October) confirming Labour government.
1975	Decisive victory of 'Yes' campaign in EEC referendum.
	Heath replaced by Margaret Thatcher as Conservative leader.
1976	Sudden resignation of Wilson; Jim Callaghan becomes prime minister.
	Financial crisis and application for large IMF loan.
1978	Callaghan faces crisis over devolution, the economy and party unity.
1979	Election victory of Thatcher.

The achievements of Harold Wilson, 1964–70

The Wilson government committed itself above all to economic success, to ending the cycle of 'Stop–Go' (see page 108) and to bringing about fundamental economic and social modernisation. Wilson believed that the Treasury was a large part of the reasons why the British economy was sluggish and unadventurous; this is why he decided to set up a new Department of Economic Affairs (DEA) under **George Brown**, aimed at enabling bolder economic policies to be pushed through. **Tony Benn** was placed in charge of the new Ministry of Technology.

Wilson believed that the Treasury was dominated by officials and advisors who would always favour cautious and traditional financial policies and that the Treasury was a large part of the reason why the British economy was sluggish and unadventurous. This is why Wilson decided to set up a new Department of Economic Affairs (DEA) under George Brown, in order to push through bolder policies. Brown was in charge of an ambitious National Economic Plan to coordinate modernisation. Tony Benn was placed in charge of the new Ministry of Technology.

However, this initiative was unsuccessful. Numerous suggestions have been made to explain this, some controversial, some widely accepted.

- There was rivalry and confusion between the Treasury and the DEA.
- George Brown was ineffectual, being erratic and inconsistent (and had a serious drink problem) and had to be shifted to the post of Foreign Secretary in 1966.
- The National Economic Plan was dropped in 1967.
- The 'establishment' – the civil service, the City, the Tory Press – placed obstacles in the path of Labour policies.

George Brown
(1914-1985)
Brown was a key Labour politician and became Deputy leader in 1960. In 1964, Wilson placed him at the head of the DEA but his position was weakened by the failure of the DEA and by the devaluation of the pound in 1967. He resigned in 1968.

Tony Benn
(1925-) Benn was formerly Lord Stansgate; he fought a campaign supporting the Peerage Act so he could give up his title and continue as an MP. He held cabinet posts between 1964 and 1979, and became known as the leader of the 'Bennite Left', Healey very nearly defeated him in the 1981 contest for the position of deputy leader.

**Michael
Cummings
cartoon
about Harold
Wilson and
the problems
with the
unions,
1969.**

- Since the 1961 application to join the EEC had failed the Labour government, badly divided about Europe, faced great difficulty making a new application for British entry.
- Wilson was indecisive, unable to control the Labour Left and obsessed with maintaining party unity.

The culmination of the disillusionment of the Labour government came in 1967. A severe balance of payments problem led to the devaluation of the pound. This was a major blow to Labour's credibility and an easy target for Tory insults about previous Labour devaluations in 1931 and 1947. The sense of economic failure was increased by the failure of Britain's application to join the EEC. Most of all, however, Wilson's position was undermined by his apparent failure to deal with the unions, and the seamen's strike of 1966 was blamed for worsening the economic situation. When Wilson attempted radical reform of industrial relations, the outcome was a damaging climbdown.

The 1968 government White Paper, 'In Place of Strife', proposed important new legal restrictions on the right to strike. **Barbara Castle**, the Employment Secretary, seemed the ideal choice to pilot through this controversial plan since she had an impeccable left-wing record and was known for her determination. However, there was strong opposition within the Labour movement, perhaps most decisively from Jim Callaghan, who argued forcefully against any confrontation with the unions. When Wilson backed off and withdrew 'In Place of Strife' in 1969, the consequences were very harmful for Labour. The issue had divided the party; Wilson appeared indecisive; letting down Barbara Castle made him seem obsessed with tactics rather than principle. Moreover, the Labour Party appeared completely dependent on the financial support from the unions and under the thumb of the union block vote.

The record of the Labour government from 1964–70 was not all failure. Important social legislation was passed in 1967 and 1968: the Abortion Act, the Sexual Offences Act and the Race Relations Act, were all key measures in modernising outdated laws and attitudes. Wilson was especially proud of the establishment of the Open University in 1969. Labour's economic difficulties were managed very effectively by the new Chancellor Roy Jenkins, who achieved a healthier balance of payments situation in time for the 1970 election. By that time, the Labour government seemed to have overcome its early mistakes and so the Conservative victory in 1970 was a surprise.

The Heath government, 1970–4

The main significance of the government of Edward Heath is to be found in the sections on Britain in Europe (pages 94–103), on the impact on the economy of the 1973 oil price crisis (page 76) and on the 'Troubles' in Northern Ireland (pages 141–144). In political terms, Heath was important for being the last of the so-called 'One Nation' Conservatives and for being the man who was defeated by Margaret Thatcher in 1975.

In fact, Heath prided himself on being a technocrat and a moderniser. He set out after his election victory with a quite radical drive for efficiency and the slogan 'No more support for lame ducks'. One of his first measures was the Industrial Relations Act (1971), which was intended to provide what 'In Place of Strife' had failed to deliver, a legal framework to regulate the trade unions and to limit strikes. However, the economic circumstances caused by the oil price crisis of 1973–4, which fuelled rising inflation, undermined his policies. His drive for improved industrial relations involved offering cooperation with the unions in return for an agreed wages policy, but this failed to convince union leaders. Heath thus found himself in a major confrontation with the miners in 1972 and again two years later.

In 1974, in a fraught atmosphere of energy crisis and **the three-day week**, Heath called a snap election on the issue of 'who governs Britain?' The result was a **hung election** after which Heath was forced to resign. He remained Party leader until 1975, just long enough to see the EEC referendum passed by a big majority, but was soon afterwards displaced in a party rebellion that made **Margaret Thatcher** leader. The Conservative Party was moving to the Right and away from consensus.

The Wilson and Callaghan governments, 1974–9

From 1974, the Labour government faced enormous problems, none of which was effectively overcome.

- Even after the October 1974 election strengthened Labour's lead over the Conservatives, Wilson had a fragile overall majority. This made party management difficult and eventually made Labour dependent on support from other parties.
- The economic effects of the oil price crisis were deep and lasting. Inflation soared, putting a huge strain on the costs of the public sector; the government was forced into spending cuts.
- Industrial relations, supposedly a great Labour strength, were virtually a repeat of the problems that had troubled Heath.
- The left wing of the Labour Party was extremely vocal, moving towards more extreme positions on public spending and foreign policy and widening party divisions that already existed in the 1960s.
- Wilson's leadership was less energetic and effective than in his first term.

The three-day week in 1973 and 1974, the Heath government was confronted by an economic crisis and a prolonged miners' strike. British industry operated on only three days per week, in order to conserve energy supplies.

The elections of 1974

February 1974

Conservative	297	38%
Labour	301	37%
Liberal	9	19%

October 1974

Conservative	277	36%
Labour	319	39%
Liberal	13	18%

KEY PERSON

Margaret Thatcher (1925-) a Conservative MP from 1959 and education secretary in the Heath cabinet 1970-74. In 1975, backed by Keith Joseph, she displaced Heath as party leader.

Labour in crisis 1976–1979

In 1976, Labour was hit by a double blow. Wilson suddenly resigned, to be replaced by Jim Callaghan, and a financial crisis hit the British economy with such force that the Labour Chancellor, Denis Healey, was forced to apply to the International Monetary Fund for a massive loan. The conditions attached to the IMF loan required major cuts in public spending and led to a sharp rise in unemployment. This enraged both the Labour left and the unions.

Jim Callaghan might in other circumstances have proved a highly successful Party leader, having wide experience and good links to all sections of the Labour movement. However, the political and economic situation he inherited was exceptional, forcing him to rely on the so-called **Lib–Lab Pact** to survive. Having hesitated to call an election in 1978 (when many commentators thought Labour might just win), Callaghan was overtaken by the 'Winter of discontent' of 1978–9 and was defeated by Mrs Thatcher.

Why did Labour lose in 1979?

There were obvious short-term reasons for Labour's defeat in 1979, specific to 1978–9: the 'Winter of Discontent', Callaghan's decision to hold back in 1978, the events of the actual election campaign. The Conservatives, for example, had great success in using modern, slick and eye-catching **advertising techniques**, especially those of the Saatchi brothers. Their most famous and effective poster was headed, 'Labour isn't working'. Other, deeper reasons included the extent of internal divisions in the Party and disillusionment among voters due to Labour's failings in government.

What happened after 1979 tended to distort the truth about the 1979 election. Indeed, a Labour defeat was not a predestined certainty; it was a close-run campaign and Callaghan might have won if he had gone for an election in 1978. Moreover, had Labour not been defeated, the internal divisions within the Party might not have run out of control as they did in the early 1980s. Secondly, the Margaret Thatcher of 1979 was not the dominating political figure she later became. Thatcher was an unknown quantity and, at that time, far from popular, even within her own party. However, in her own mind she was committed to breaking with the past. From 1979, the intention of Mrs Thatcher was to make sure that the post-war consensus was removed.

SECTION 2

Was there a 'Sixties social revolution'?

The concept of social revolution is not universally accepted. For many historians, change and continuity are impossible to separate, and, in any case, the causes of change are often subtle and slow to take effect. But for others, such as **Eric Hobsbawm** and, above all, the social historian **Arthur Marwick**, the Sixties was indeed a time of social and cultural revolution, not least because of the perceptions of those who lived through what *felt* like a unique decade and its symbolic 'year of youth' in 1968.

WHAT IS THE BASIS OF CLAIMS THAT THE 1960S WITNESSED A SOCIAL REVOLUTION?

Arguments for a social revolution

Marwick provided the classic definition of the Sixties phenomenon. First, he placed it in a very specific timescale, starting in about 1958 and coming to an end in 1973, with the end of the long post-war boom. He then set out his sixteen 'characteristics of a unique era'.

1   The formation of new subcultures opposed to established society.
2   An outburst of individualism.
3   The emergence of youth culture.
4   Technological advances, including television and mass air travel.
5   The growth of 'world news' and international media images.
6   International cultural exchange, through tourism and popular music.
7   Improvements in material life and the 'consumer society'.
8   Upheavals in race, class and family relationships.
9   Sexual liberation and the rise of permissiveness.
10   Greater freedoms in fashion and self-expression.
11   Rock music as a kind of international language.
12   Revolutionary tendencies in elite culture, for example, literature and music.
13   Liberal tolerance inherited from the previous generation.
14   A 'conservative backlash' from the older generation.
15   A new concern with civil rights.
16   Multiculturalism and the recognition of ethnic diversity.

This brief summary does not do full justice to Marwick's long and complex book, *The Sixties* (1998), which does not only concern Britain but tries to explain the Sixties in terms of western society as a whole.

KEY TEXTS

Eric Hobsbawm
Age of Extremes: The Short Twentieth Century, 1914–91 (Abacus, 1994)

Arthur Marwick
The Sixties (Oxford University Press, 1998)

Marwick is also very forthright in assessing the causes of this revolution. First, there were what he terms *structural* changes: the affluence of the post-war boom; the impact of the Welfare State and improved health standards; the wartime baby boom and the rising proportion of teenagers in society; technological advances accelerating change. Then, there were *ideological* changes: changing attitudes to the role of women; a greater focus on equality after the 'People's War'; new ideas developed in politics, sociology and philosophy.

These causes include factors originating well before the Sixties, especially those growing out of the Second World War. Nevertheless, Marwick's theory assumes that it was in the 1960s that these factors came to the forefront of peoples minds – that any revolutionary changes up to 1945 were delayed until the right context for their release.

Critics of the theory of social revolution

Marwick has made a powerful case but there are equally powerful arguments that there was more continuity than change – that the Sixties social revolution was a myth.

- Social change cannot be neatly compartmentalised but is always part of a long-term ebb and flow. The advance of women, for example, began before the First World War, was accelerated by the Second World War, and was still not complete in the 1990s.
- Social change in the 1960s was not universal: where it happened at all, it concerned mostly the educated middle classes; there were massive variations according to age, class or region.
- The social and cultural trends of the Sixties did not last. By 1979, Margaret Thatcher was winning power with a political style that looked very much like that of the socially conservative 1950s. The Conservative Party held power for 22 of the 28 years between 1970 and 1997.

This is a debate in which there can be no definitive answer. A general theory such as Marwick's is ultimately subjective and matched by so many exceptions and alternative explanations that it can never be proved. All that the A2 level student of history can do is to analyse the social and cultural changes of the 1960s and come to an individual judgement as to whether these changes outweighed the continuities and can therefore justify the label 'social revolution'.

HOW EXTENSIVE WERE THE SOCIAL AND CULTURAL CHANGES THAT TOOK PLACE BETWEEN THE LATE 1950S AND THE EARLY 1970S?

When Macmillan led the Conservative Party to a thumping victory in the 1959 general election, he did so on the back of consumer prosperity and the slogan 'You've never had it so good'. A famous Vicky cartoon at the time had Macmillan addressing a roomful of consumer goods, such as televisions and washing machines, telling them: 'Well, boys, we fought a good campaign.' However, between 1959 and 1964, the Conservative party was overtaken by new social and political developments. These included:

- the re-emergence of the Labour Party, with Harold Wilson as leader from 1963, offering a youthful and dynamic contrast to Harold Macmillan and Alec Douglas-Hume
- the development of anti-establishment attitudes: some were rooted in the protests against the Suez invasion, others reflected in the rise of the Campaign for Nuclear Disarmament (CND)
- a reaction against the 'boring' prosperity of the 1950s boom. Some historians argue that the real impact of the 1963 Profumo Affair was not in its political or its security issues, but in reflecting a revolutionary new attitude towards matters of sexual behaviour, including the willingness to publish the details. It has been plausibly claimed that Labour won in 1964 because they were more in tune with radical social and cultural changes.

KEY TEXT

B. Pimlott,
Wilson (1992)

Changing social attitudes

There were significant cultural developments in the early 1960s that reflected the new mood. Satire came into fashion through the press, with *Private Eye*, and through television, with *That Was The Week That Was*, launched by the BBC in 1962. In 1960, D.H. Lawrence's long-banned novel *Lady Chatterley's Lover* was brought out in a paperback edition by Penguin; the publishers were prosecuted for 'publishing obscene material'. The failure of the prosecution was a landmark in the liberalisation of attitudes to censorship and to sexual matters. Similar attempts to censor the theatre also failed; London stage productions featured swearing, nudity and previously taboo issues such as homosexuality.

By 1962, the Beatles had begun their phenomenal rise, marking a major change in the world of popular music. Eric Hobsbawm believes that a key factor in the surge in popular music was the emergence of affluent teenagers who had the spending power to fuel the huge sales of pop records. (Students need to be very careful in assessing the 'revolutionary' aspects of popular music in the Sixties. Bill Haley's *Rock Around the Clock* and Elvis Presley both belonged to the mid-1950s. In the same way, the so-called 'angry young men', playwrights such as John Osborne, made their first impact well before 1960.)

Another sphere affecting social change and the new youth culture was the expansion of higher education. In the 1960s, 22 new universities were founded with a huge increase in the numbers of students. Many of these students were the first members of their families ever to go to university, or to leave home before marriage. The experiences of this new generation of students had a huge influence on a wide range of social issues, from soft drugs to sexual freedoms, from feminism to anti-war protests. The Sixties was also the decade of the comprehensive school. Under both Conservative and Labour Education Ministers (including in the early 1970s one called Margaret Thatcher) there was a switch away from grammar and secondary modern schools to the comprehensive model.

Social change was also visible in legislation. Under the Labour government after 1964, especially influenced by a reform-minded Home Secretary, Roy Jenkins, the law was liberalised in respect of abortion, homosexuality and divorce. It is difficult from the perspective of the early twenty-first century to appreciate what a huge change, these legal reforms represented. Abortion had been illegal and unmarried mothers were stigmatised; one of the social evils of the 1950s was the high number of back-street abortions. Homosexuality was a crime as well as a social taboo. It led to **ruined careers** and quite frequently to instances of blackmail. The Abortion Law was passed in 1967; the Wolfenden Report of 1965 opened the way for same-sex relationships 'between consenting adults over 21'.

The 'year of youth'

The culmination of the Sixties 'revolution' came in 1968: the 'year of youth'. Anti-nuclear and anti-Vietnam War protest reached a peak in huge demonstrations outside the US Embassy in Grosvenor Square. Radios were full of the sounds of Bob Dylan, and the Rolling Stones. There was hardly a student in the land who did not have a poster of **Che Guevara** on the bedroom wall. Strongly influenced by the wave of student unrest which had begun in **Paris** in May, universities such as East Anglia and the London School of Economics were taken over by student sit-ins.

On the London stage, the pop musical *Hair* featured full-frontal nudity while *Oh! Calcutta* took to swear words with enthusiasm. 1968 was also when colour television came into British homes; TV in colour, not least *advertising* in colour, had a big effect in accelerating the consumer society and its cultural side effects.

Was there a 'Sixties social revolution'?   91

Such a catalogue of social and cultural change provides very convincing evidence of a social revolution, both in fundamental 'new' changes and in the speeding up of changes already in motion. One key piece of evidence supporting the Marwick view is the fear and loathing that was revealed in the backlash against the new 'permissive society'. Church leaders tended to be anxious, trying to 'understand' the younger generation, but there was a tide of angry denunciations in the pages of several newspapers, symbolised by **Mary Whitehouse** .

This backlash can, of course, be used to prove either that there was no real social revolution (because the backlash stopped it) or that indeed there *was* a social revolution (that is why the backlash was so intense).

1956	First Eurovision Song Contest; Elvis Presley becomes a teen idol after the release of *Heartbreak Hotel*.
1957	First stereo LPs released.
1958	Race riots in Nottingham and Notting Hill; advent of Mods and Rockers.
1959	The launch of the Mini; ***Room At The Top***.
1960	Trial of *Lady Chatterley's Lover*; the start of the fashion for mini-skirts; ***Saturday Night and Sunday Morning***.
1961	Success of the satirical revue, *Beyond the Fringe*.
1962	First colour supplement issued with *The Sunday Times*.
1963	The Profumo Affair; First hit, *Come On,* for the Rolling Stones; Robbins Report on the expansion of higher education.
1964	Labour election victory.
1965	Government Circular 10/65, calling for comprehensive schools; the Beatles awarded MBEs.
1966	England's victory in the World Cup.
1967	Abortion Act; decriminalisation of homosexuality; *Sergeant Pepper's Lonely Hearts Club Band* released by the Beatles.
1968	First mass sales of colour TV sets; student sit-in at LSE; anti-war demonstrations in Grosvenor Square; South Africa cricket tour cancelled due to anti-apartheid protests.
1969	Abolition of capital punishment; reform of the divorce laws; first broadcast of *Monty Python's Flying Circus*.
1970	Equal Pay Act.
1971	Release of Stanley Kubrick's *A Clockwork Orange*.
1972	Launch of the magazines *Cosmopolitan* and *Spare Rib*.
1973	OPEC oil price crisis marks the end of the long post-war boom.

A chronology of social and cultural changes, 1956–73.

Mary Whitehouse started a National Viewers and Listeners Association to push the media (and especially the BBC) into cleaning up the 'moral filth' that was poisoning the airwaves.

KEY FACT

Room At The Top, Saturday Night and Sunday Morning were hit films that helped to establish a trend in films based on gritty urban realism. They were set against the background of the industrial North.

HEINEMANN ADVANCED HISTORY

WHAT WERE THE MOST IMPORTANT CAUSES OF SOCIAL AND CULTURAL CHANGE?

It is difficult to separate the symptoms of social change from what caused social change to happen. Television, provided a mirror in which social change could be observed; but television was itself a massive factor in bringing about change. The same could be said for popular music, or mass tourism, or car ownership, all of which both reflected changes that had taken place and helped to cause or accelerate change.

Causal factors

- **Affluence.** The consumer prosperity of the 1950s was a key factor for example, the availability of consumer goods and in teenage spending power.
- **Television.** Mass television ownership enabled fashions and social trends to spread rapidly.
- **Education.** The emergence of comprehensive schools and the expansion of higher education led to greater social mobility.
- **Immigration.** The arrival of immigrants from the **New Commonwealth**, which began with the *Empire Windrush* in 1948, made Britain a multi-cultural society in the 1960s.
- **Government legislation.** Legal reforms passed by the first Wilson government, 1964–70, had an important effect on personal freedom.
- **The legacy of the Second World War.** This continued to promote ideas of equality and approval of the Welfare State.

CONCLUSION

Perhaps the best way of assessing the extent and significance of the Sixties social revolution is to analyse how deep and lasting its effects were. However, this is extremely difficult: from what standpoint should 'afterwards' be judged? If the basis for analysis is chosen as the 1980s, the Thatcher Years could be seen as the reversal of what had gone before. If the standpoint is that of the educated professional middle classes, the extent of change is much greater. Seen from a countryside or working-class perspective, change might appear slow or non-existent.

There was undoubtedly a wave of significant social and cultural change in the Sixties. 1968 represents a genuine landmark year in the history and culture of Britain and most of the western world. Nevertheless, continuity was always there. One form of continuity is relatively easy to identify – the idea that changes started earlier than 1960 and carried on after 1970. However, it is more important to recognise continuity in the sense of change not having much of an impact at all. There was not much of a social revolution happening at, for example, the Women's Institute flower show in Dunster, the hunt in Northamptonshire, or among the men playing dominoes in the Working Man's Club in Rochdale.

KEY TERM

New Commonwealth countries were those (thus non-white) countries who had achieved independence since 1945. The 'Old Commonwealth' (thus white) countries were the original Dominions such as Canada and Australia.

Why was Europe such a difficult issue for post-war Britain?

The question of British involvement in the process of European integration was never satisfactorily resolved at any time in the post-war period. The European issue continues to dominate British politics into the twenty-first century, with Blair's Labour government still hesitant over **the euro**, and apparently the Conservative Party close to political paralysis because of unbridgeable divisions.

PHASES OF EUROPEAN INTEGRATION

There have been several distinct phases in the British relationship with Europe since the Second World War.

- In the first phase, from 1950–1 until the establishment of the EEC at the Treaty of Rome in 1957, Britain chose to stand aside from European integration. At this time, a leading British role in Europe was there for the taking had British politicians wished it.
- In the second phase, from 1958–70, the issue of Britain in Europe was dominated by the personality of President Charles de Gaulle. Two applications were made for British entry to the EEC, first by Macmillan and the Conservatives in 1961, then by Wilson and Labour in 1967. Both applications failed, largely but not only because of de Gaulle's veto see pages 98–99.
- In the third phase, 1970–9, British entry to the EEC was finally achieved in 1973 by a strongly Europhile Conservative prime minister, Edward Heath, following the resignation and death of President de Gaulle. EEC membership was later confirmed by the 1975 referendum held under the Labour prime minister, Harold Wilson, which predicted a 2:1 majority.
- In the fourth phase, from 1979–97, the apparent finality of the 1975 referendum proved to be illusory. As moves were made towards closer integration, so the Conservative 'yes vote' under Thatcher and Major both became increasingly divided and the issue of Europe became more and more controversial, not least because of the aggressively Euro-sceptic line taken by sections of the national press. What would be the outcome of the fifth phase, following the Labour victory of 1997 and the launch of the Euro, without Britain, in 1999, remained uncertain.

Making objective historical judgements about this long-running and complex saga is exceptionally difficult. The controversy is very subjective: is closer European integration 'a good thing' or not? Few of the political and journalistic contributions to the debate have been balanced or objective; most have arranged the evidence to fit a predetermined stance. Many widely used terms and definitions turn out to be vague and imprecise, such as the term 'Euro-sceptic', which can mean almost anything from 'pro-European but doubtful about the single currency' to 'let's pull out of Europe altogether'.

There have also been significant changes over time. What was at stake in the 1950s, a Common Market, became by the 1990s a much more political project. Between the Second World War and 1975, it was in the Labour Party that the most strenuous opposition to European integration was found; from the 1980s, the majority of the doubters were in the Conservative Party. There were also more serious divisions *within* the major parties than between them. In the 1975 referendum, both the 'Yes' and the 'No' campaigns involved some unlikely pairings from the Left and Right of the political spectrum, with **Willie Whitelaw** and Roy Jenkins as allies in one camp and Tony Benn and Enoch Powell as allies in the other.

THE EUROPEAN DEBATE

Making due allowance for changes over time, it may be useful to identify the personalities, groups and issues associated with the two sides of the divide. However, it is very important to recognise that the issue of Britain in Europe has never been clear-cut. Committed Europhiles and, even more so, committed Euro-sceptics have acted on strong convictions and have frequently polarised the debate; only a minority of British opinion has ever been fixed and immovable on the issue. Most of the electorate, perhaps most individual people, have responded with mixed feelings, capable of switching from one position to another; the true believers represent a vocal minority.

The case for Britain in Europe

- **Economic realism.** Many, such as Harold Macmillan, became convinced that Britain's economic future depended on Europe. This feeling was strengthened by the rapid successes of the common market economies in the 1950s.
- **Retreat from empire.** Many who originally wished to make the most of Britain's links with the empire and Commonwealth decided, after the 1956 Suez Crisis, that this was not possible and that Britain would be stronger as part of Europe.

- **Concerns for peace and stability in Europe.** Many traditionalists, such as Willie Whitelaw, would have been natural Euro-sceptics on most grounds but became totally committed to the 'Yes' camp in 1975 because of the conviction that integration would end centuries of European conflict.
- **The Cold War.** US foreign policy encouraged closer British involvement with allies in Europe as a way of building up the defence of western capitalism.
- **Edward Heath.** Heath was the chief negotiator in the first British application to join the EEC in 1961–3, the prime minister who took Britain into the EEC in 1973, and a key figure in the 1975 referendum.
- **Roy Jenkins.** Labour Chancellor until 1970, Jenkins resigned from the Shadow Cabinet in 1972 and from the Labour Party altogether in 1981, partly because of growing disillusionment with anti-European trends within Labour.
- **Businessmen.** Many were convinced that British integration in Europe would benefit the economy.

The case against Britain in Europe

- **Fear of capitalism.** Many on the Labour Left, including Tony Benn and a number of trade union leaders, saw the EEC as a 'capitalist club'. They wanted to end the Cold War and reduce US influence in Europe.
- **Fear of socialism.** Many on the right wing of the Conservative Party (including, by the late 1980s, Margaret Thatcher) saw the European Union and its Social Chapter as being a corporatist organisation, dedicated to government controls and a socialist view of economic affairs. Many regarded the US economic model as more desirable – freer and more dynamic.
- **Concerns for national sovereignty.** This was an issue that united Left and Right; for example, the Labour politician Peter Shore and many right-wing newspaper editors agreed that Britain should not surrender power from the British Parliament to 'unelected bureaucrats in Brussels', nor from British judges to the European Court.
- **Nostalgia for the Empire and Commonwealth.** These influences were especially marked in the formative period of 1945–57, when it was believed that Britain simply could not betray its traditional ties (and recent wartime allies) in favour of Europe.
- **The legacy of the Second World War.** This involved both the feeling that Europe *needed* greater integration but Britain did not ('they lost, we won') and a persistent **anti-German sentiment** hanging over from wartime stereotypes.
- **Businessmen.** Many are convinced that European integration has been and would continue to be harmful to the economy.

KEY THEMES

Common Agricultural Policy this was originally very successful in securing adequate food supplies after the shortages of the post-war years. But the subsidies to farmers distorted the market in agricultural production, creating embarrassing surpluses known as 'food mountains'.

KEY TERM

European Coal and Steel Community was proposed by the Schuman Plan in 1950. It integrated French and German heavy industry. This close partnership provided the basis for the EEC to develop later in the 1950s.

- **Criticisms of Europe.** These include allegations of corruption and inefficiency, especially the long-lasting failure to reform the **Common Agricultural Policy**.

The arguments set out here for and against European integration are only a selection from countless examples; nonetheless, they provide sufficient evidence of the many contradictions, shifts over time and the different levels on which the European issue has been fought – economic, political and emotional. Historians can quite easily assemble a range of relevant factors, but differentiating between them and fitting them into a coherent overall argument presents a formidable task.

WHY DID BRITAIN NOT BECOME A FOUNDER MEMBER OF THE EEC IN THE 1950S WHEN IT WOULD HAVE BEEN EASY TO DO SO?
Post-war relationships

The foundation of the EEC began formally in 1955–7 with the Messina Conference and the Treaty of Rome; but its origins went back to the **European Coal and Steel Community** (ECSC) in 1950–1. The ECSC grew out of extensive preparations that began almost as soon as the Second World War ended. In this respect, the real drive behind the plans for European integration came from the appalling situation of Western Europe in 1946–7. There was economic chaos and very real fear of a communist takeover in Italy or France. There was also a deep conviction among many French politicians that the generations of French–German hostility had to stop. In continental Europe, therefore, there were powerful forces pushing towards integration.

In Britain after the war, however, the sense of separateness from Europe widened. Why would 'victorious' Britain want to join with ravaged former enemies? At the same time, Britain had drawn much closer to the USA. This was a time when the 'special relationship' did indeed seem special and when all things American were desirable. British policy-makers were quite keen to encourage European integration from the sidelines but had no wish to become participants. In 1949, a government committee concluded that: 'Our policy should be to assist Europe to recover. But in no circumstances must we assist them beyond the point where our assistance would leave us too weak to be a worthwhile ally for the USA. In the last resort, we cannot rely on European countries.'

Doubts about British involvement in Europe applied to both main political parties. Winston Churchill was enthusiastic about closer cooperation between the European states but saw Britain in a different, bigger role, strengthening links between Europe, the USA and the

Commonwealth. In this respect, Britain was to be 'with Europe but not of it'. Clement Attlee, who remained Labour leader until 1955, was even more certain that Britain should stay out of the developing ECSC. He was concerned about protecting the coal industry, recently nationalised by Labour, and with the issue of sovereignty. He stated in 1951 that Labour 'was not prepared to accept the principle that the most vital economic force of the country should be handed over to an authority that is utterly undemocratic and is responsible to nobody'.

Attlee's viewpoint reflects a fundamental sticking point that remained strong on both Left and Right throughout the post-war years. Along with many other concerns, such as the enormously complicated issue of how to marry membership of a European market with Britain's trade links to the rest of the world, it did much to ensure that Britain continued to stand aside. Nevertheless, it is possible to argue that the key factor was the persistence of unrealistic ambitions for Britain to maintain its role as a world power. Once these ambitions were exposed as illusions, many came to believe that the decision to stand aside had been a big mistake. The disillusionment, brought about by the Suez fiasco in 1956, came just too late to alter the British stance towards the **Treaty of Rome**.

WHY DID THE BRITISH APPLICATIONS FOR EEC ENTRY FAIL IN THE 1960S?

Historians rarely conclude that there is a simple answer to a complex question, but Britain's failure to join the EEC in the 1960s may be an exceptional case. Up to 1957, Britain stayed on the European sidelines even though the door was held open for British entry almost to the last moment, both at **the Messina Conference in 1955** and in the run-up to signing the **Treaty of Rome**. Then, in 1958, just when the Conservative government was reassessing the situation and coming to the conclusion that Britain had 'missed the European bus', Charles de Gaulle became President of France. It can be convincingly argued that it was de Gaulle's dominant personality and political influence that kept Britain out of Europe until 1973.

The role of de Gaulle

President de Gaulle had strong motivations for blocking British entry.

- By the late 1950s, French–German cooperation was well established; de Gaulle was determined to strengthen and defend this vital relationship.
- de Gaulle was genuinely worried about the 'Atlantic' outlook of British policy. He feared that Britain would be an unreliable European partner, a Trojan horse for US influence in Europe.

EVENTS

The Messina Conference, 1955 this conference established the final form of the EEC, later ratified by the 1957 Treaty of Rome. Britain sent observers but opted out of joining 'The Six'.

KEY TREATY

The Treaty of Rome, 1957 was the legal basis of the EEC, signed by 'the six' – the founder states of France, Germany, Italy and the Benelux countries.

- de Gaulle wanted to push forward an **ambitious Gaullist foreign policy** and saw Britain as a rival who might obstruct this.
- de Gaulle was also extremely touchy about what he saw as his humiliating treatment by his wartime allies (he was especially bitter about US President Roosevelt). It has been seriously suggested that de Gaulle's main motivation in 1963 was personal pique against the 'Anglo-Saxons'.

Although there were many other factors to explain the rejection of Britain's 1961 application, the circumstantial evidence is strong. Before the arrival of de Gaulle, the European door was open; with de Gaulle there, it was shut. While de Gaulle remained French President, both British applications were refused; almost as soon as he was replaced by **Pompidou**, British entry to the EEC became possible. It may also be significant that the many difficult issues and obstacles in the way of British entry in 1961 *were* overcome. De Gaulle only came into the open and used the French veto in 1963 because the dogged negotiations led by Edward Heath had unexpectedly succeeded when de Gaulle had expected them to fail.

The significance of failure to join in 1961–3

The fact that the British application to join the EEC failed in 1961–3 may be of long-term significance. Macmillan had won a convincing election success in 1959. Moreover, the Labour opposition was weak and increasingly divided, whereas Macmillan had wide acceptance among Conservatives for his policy even if this acceptance did not necessarily mean complete enthusiasm. The bulk of the Conservative Party (and of the national press) were convinced, both for domestic economic concerns and for the sake of Britain's foreign position, that membership of the EEC had become essential to British interests. Had Macmillan's application succeeded, it is likely that a national consensus about Europe would have been consolidated relatively securely.

By the time Britain applied again, in 1967, Harold Wilson was already walking a tactical tightrope between the warring factions of the Labour movement. By the time Britain joined in 1973, the years of prosperity in the long post-war boom were coming to an end and what Heath called the 'full-hearted acceptance' of Europe was more difficult to achieve. On political and economic grounds, 1973 may have been too late.

WHY WAS THE ISSUE OF BRITAIN IN EUROPE NOT FINALLY RESOLVED BETWEEN 1973 AND 1975?

Edward Heath's main achievement in politics was the success of Britain's third application to join the EEC in 1973. At the time, Heath was sure that the success would be final, enabling Britain to make up for lost time and to play a leading European role. However, 1973 proved to be no more than one more episode in an unfinished story. Ironically, in view of the bitter divisions that affected Heath's party in later years, it was not the Conservatives but the Labour Party that undermined the 'finality' of 1973.

The 1975 referendum

Harold Wilson returned to power in 1974 with a small majority, a badly splintered party and a difficult economic situation. Wilson was first and foremost a tactician, aiming to preserve Labour unity without confrontation. His device for getting round Labour divisions over Europe was to promise a national referendum. Outwardly, this was extremely successful, both in party terms and for the European issue. The fact that the 1975 referendum was won by a decisive two-third majority seemingly demonstrated national acceptance. Wilson did not take part in the campaign and thus avoided falling out with either wing of his Party. The fact that the 'Yes' campaign combined a cross-section of leading politicians from the three main parties (such as Heath and Whitelaw, Jenkins and Healey, and the Liberals) seemed to finally resolve the issue once and for all.

In reality, the 1975 referendum simply perpetuated the uncertainties over Europe. The 'No' campaign was heavily defeated but actually gained impetus, not least because it enabled anti-European elements in the Conservative Party to assert themselves without the danger of being disloyal to the Party. Tony Benn wrote in 1979, 'It is no part of the democratic debate that you have to accept any defeat as final.' Alongside Benn and the Labour Left were right-wing Conservatives such as Enoch Powell. The 1975 referendum enabled them to rehearse the arguments that would grow stronger after 1979 rather than die away as had been hoped

WHY DID BRITAIN'S RELATIONS WITH EUROPE REMAIN CONTROVERSIAL AND UNRESOLVED BETWEEN 1979 AND 1997?
Developments under Thatcher

Margaret Thatcher was by no means as anti-European when she came to power in 1979. She had been part of Heath's Cabinet when EEC entry was secured in 1973. During the 1980s, many of her key ministers, like **Geoffrey Howe** and **Nigel Lawson**, were strongly Europhile. While in office, Thatcher passed more laws binding Britain closer to Europe than any leader before or since. Yet by 1990, Europe was causing considerable tensions within the Conservative government and once out of office

KEY PLACE

Brussels is the headquarters of the European Commission, thus 'Brussels' became a term of abuse for Eurosceptics.

KEY PEOPLE

Jacques Delors (1925-) the Secretary of the European Commission, committed to closer integration. He became a target for Mrs Thatcher and right-wing Eurosceptic newspapers, famously in the 1988 *Sun* headline: 'Up yours, Delors!'

Norman Tebbit (1925-) a committed supporter of Thatcher against the traditional elements in the Tory party.

TERMS

'Drys' and **'wets'** 'Wets' a term for those who were cautious about the effects on society of free-market philosophy; 'Drys' were those in favour of monetarism, however harsh the social consequences.

Thatcher became stridently anti-**Brussels**. Very different possible explanations may account for this.

- Thatcher changed over time; as she became more powerful and less tolerant of her colleagues, she let her natural instincts come through, especially her negative perceptions of Germany and the Germans.
- Thatcher herself would claim that *she* did not change but Europe did. In her view, she had been always been in favour of economic integration and the single market but, in the 1980s, Europe was moving in the direction of a federal superstate, led by her *bete noire* **Jacques Delors**.
- The Conservative Party changed. The Thatcher governments reflected a new breed of middle-class politics: more so-called '**drys**' and fewer '**wets**'; more people such as **Norman Tebbit** and fewer traditional 'One Nation' Tories. The Conservative politicians Thatcher fought hardest against (for example Heath, Heseltine and Howe) happened to be the Europhile ones.
- The public mood changed. The national press, especially the papers owned by Rupert Murdoch and Conrad Black, promoted a backlash against Europe.

Divisions under Major

Whatever the reasons, the Conservatives after Thatcher's fall were more fiercely at odds over Europe than they had ever been while she was prime minister. This made the position of **John Major** immensely difficult. Almost the first big problem he faced after winning the 1992 election was to sign the **Maastricht Treaty**, which turned the European Community into the European Union. In this, Major was carrying through and completing policies already well under way in Thatcher's time (he also managed to secure a British opt-out from the **Social Chapter**, which was at least as much as Thatcher could have achieved). Major came under fierce attack from the 'Maastricht rebels'; soon afterwards, the ERM crisis of 1993 (see pages 129–130) further intensified Conservative divisions.

For the rest of his time in office, Major was dogged by constant criticism from the 'Euro-sceptic tendency'. While the modernisation of New Labour produced discipline and impeccable party unity instead of the old Labour feuds, the Conservative party under Major became almost a continuous battlefield over Europe. In Parliament, the Liberal leader Paddy Ashdown witheringly described the Conservatives: 'This was the heart-of-Europe Party; is now the edge-of-Europe Party; and will soon become the out-of-Europe Party'. By the time of the 1997 election, the Referendum Party had been formed, financed by the anti-Europe billionaire Lord Goldsmith. Its candidates generally did badly but took sufficient votes away from the Conservatives to make Major's defeat at the 1997 general election, even worse than it was already destined to be.

Why was Europe such a difficult issue for post-war Britain?   101

What were the reasons for the 'Eurosceptic' backlash?

Outwardly, it was somewhat surprising that the campaign against the single currency, the Euro, was so intense. After all, Heath's government had piloted through the decimalisation of the currency in 1971, something that might have been expected to be even more emotive. Why did the Euro-sceptic tide run so strongly in the late 1990s?

- Perhaps it did not: the Conservatives were heavily defeated in 1997, and again in 2001 when 'saving the pound' was its trump card. Perhaps the Euro sceptics were but a loud minority (and perhaps the civil war in the Conservative Party was more about Thatcher than Europe).
- Perhaps the end of the Cold War removed a fundamental reason for Western European unity; the collapse of the Soviet Bloc made the capitalist free-for-all seem more progressive than supranational organisations.
- Perhaps the 50th anniversary of the Second World War made public opinion excessively conscious of the dark side of European (and specifically German) history, as well as Britain's 'island mentality'.
- Perhaps the anti-European voices were correct: the 1990s, specifically the Maastricht Treaty, may have been the point at which the wider public realised what European integration was leading towards. Perhaps there really was a majority agreeing with the verdict of Hugh Gaitskell, who said in 1963, 'Entry (to the EEC) means the end of Britain as a nation; we become no more than Texas or California in the USA. It means the end of a thousand years of history.'
- Perhaps furious debates over Europe will die away with the generation of the Second World War and British illusions of empire. Gaitskell was from that generation, so were Churchill, Attlee, Thatcher and Benn.

Political cartoon showing John Major and Norman Tebbit fighting it out 'Aye and No' over the Maastricht Treaty, 1992.

"ONCE MORE UNTO THE BREACH, DEAR FRIENDS..."

KEY PERSON

John Major (1943-) was little-known until he suddenly rose to high cabinet posts in 1987-90. Succeeded Mrs Thatcher as prime minister, largely because Tory right wings wanted to block Michael Heseltine. Major took Britain into the ERM in 1990, and later negotiated British acceptance of the Maastricht Treaty.

KEY TREATY

Maastricht Treaty (1991) a big step towards greater European integration. John Major negotiated opt-out clauses for Britain from the Social Chapter and from the plans for a Single Currency. From 1992, Maastricht was bitterly attacked by Eurosceptic rebels such as Ian Duncan-Smith.

KEY TERM

Social Chapter measures to protect workers in Europe. Britain opted out for concerns that restrictions would damage economic growth.

KEY ACT

Single European Act (1986) established the single market, and adopted the European flag.

CONCLUSION

In the early twenty-first century, the answers to such questions over Europe belong more to politics and current affairs than to history. Historians have no way of predicting whether Britain will once again, as in the 1950s, 'miss the European bus'. Neither can they anticipate whether the successes of European integration since the 1950s, rooted in the specific circumstances of the Cold War world, will prove to be of relevance in the future.

Yet there is one present-day contradiction that is genuinely historical: whatever the future relationships between Britain and Europe, British life has never been more European than in the late 1990s. British generations brought up on mass tourism and accustomed to the influx of migrants and refugees (not to mention European football) are accustomed to drinking red wine and cafe latte to eating pasta and driving German cars. The daily lives of British citizens reflect a thousand other European influences from tourism to furniture to supermarkets. Fifty years after opting out of the Treaty of Rome, Britain is undeniably 'of Europe'.

Landmarks of Britain's relationship with Europe, 1951–99.

1951	Formation of the European Coal and Steel Community (ECSC).
1955	Messina Conference.
1957	Treaty of Rome.
1958	Establishment of the French Fifth Republic under de Gaulle.
1961	First British application for membership of the European Economic Community (EEC).
1963	Rejection of Britain's application to join the EEC after de Gaulle's veto.
1967	Failure of application to join the EEC by Wilson's Labour government.
1969	Resignation of de Gaulle.
1973	Britain accepted as one of three new members of the EEC.
1975	Referendum in Britain to confirm membership of the EEC; two-thirds majority in favour.
1975	Heath replaced by Thatcher as Conservative leader.
1986	**Single European Act.**
1990	German reunification; fall of Margaret Thatcher.
1992	European Union established by the Maastricht Treaty.
1995	Conservative leadership election called by John Major.
1997	Conservative government heavily defeated in general election.
1999	The single currency (euro) launched without British involvement.

SECTION 4

Was there continuous economic decline in Britain during the second half of the twentieth century?

INTRODUCTION

Historians must be careful with self-evident truths. Sometimes a self-evident truth is more evident than it is true; very often one self-evident truth collides head-on with another one going in the opposite direction. This is particularly so in the assessment of the post-war British economy.

For many historians and economists it is 'obvious' that there was a continuous economic decline. Travelling round Britain in the early twenty-first century, it is easy to find whole areas of dereliction and disuse where there used to be a humming industrial powerhouse: shipbuilding in the North East, coal mining in South Wales, metal-bashing industries in the West Midlands. After the Second World War, Britain's position in international economic league tables slipped downwards. British industry lacked competitiveness; there were numerous high-profile failures in managing big projects. Many economic analysts defined the 'British disease' of low productivity and low investment. Such fears for the British economy reached a peak in the 1970s and early 1980s, after the OPEC oil price crisis of 1973–4.

Against this, however, it is equally 'obvious' that post-war Britain experienced a period of sustained prosperity and ever-rising living standards. For historians like **Peter Hennessy** or Larry Elliott and Dan Atkinson, the years from 1950–73 represented a 'Golden Age' – high growth rates, full employment, massive advances in welfare – in stark contrast to the strains of the war and the dreadful memories of the 1930s. Despite the downturn of the 1970s, living standards continued to rise. At the end of the 1990s, almost any measurement of economic well-being showed huge advances since 1950, above all in consumer goods and the ownership of cars and houses. The post-war period was a generation of rising expectations. It was probably a time of greater prosperity for a greater proportion of the people than at any stage in the history of the nation. Britain, along with western Europe, experienced an 'economic miracle'.

Deciding between these 'truths' is a difficult task in itself. It is also complicated by two key debates.

KEY TEXT

S Pollard
The Development of the British Economy 1914–1990 (1992)

KEY TEXT

Peter Hennessy
Never Again (1992)

L. Elliott and D. Atkinson *The Age of Insecurity* (1998)

Key debates

The first issue is political and ideological. Economic assessments of post-war Britain are invariably based on attitudes towards a political ideal. For historians like **Correlli Barnett** and those of a Thatcherite outlook, the post-war era was a failure marked by excessive social spending, by kow-towing to the trade unions, by a failure to match the US model of free enterprise and by a lack of competitiveness. In their eyes, 1979 was a landmark when the post-war failures were confronted and Mrs Thatcher began to save the country from the 'British disease'. For historians like Eric Hobsbawm, however, 1979 was a different sort of turning point altogether, marking the stage at which the successful post-war consensus about the mixed economy was needlessly and harmfully smashed, leading to the destruction of British industry and to dangerous divisions in society – to 'private affluence and public squalor'.

The second issue is the European perspective. Britain's economic decline was relative: the economy grew but in the context of a general 'economic miracle' across the developed world. In Europe terms, Britain fell behind the faster economic growth of Germany and France, even Italy.

Assessing relative success or relative decline is difficult and is made even more tricky by conflicting interpretations of Britain's relationship with European integration. For many observers, it appears obvious that the British economy suffered badly from failing to enter the EEC at the beginning. The period while Britain was outside Europe, 1951–1973, was precisely the period of the economic miracle. When Britain finally joined the EEC in 1973, it was just in time for the recession that followed the oil price crisis, having missed a golden opportunity to share in Europe's time of greatest growth and success. Such a view, however, would be strenuously attacked by Euro-sceptics and those who are convinced that the collectivist European approach to the so-called 'social market economy' has damaged Britain's economic position.

Key factors, 1951–97

A number of key factors characterised the period from 1951–97. Firstly Britain had achieved a substantial economic recovery between 1947 and 1951, but there were many burdens of debt hanging over from the war. There were also many structural problems in the staple industries going back to the interwar period. Secondly the 1944 Bretton Woods Conference led to stability in exchange rates and to general acceptance of **Keynesian economic principles** in western economies. British foreign policy, pursuing a world role, led to relatively high defence spending, far higher, than Germany or Japan.

KEY TEXTS

C. Barnett *The Lost Victory* (1995)

In this book, and in *The Audit of War*, Barnett argued strongly that Britain's economy had been badly mismanaged since 1945.

E. Hobsbawm *Interesting Times* (2002)

KEY FACT

Keynesian economic principles were based on the assumption that public spending was necessary to inflate the economy in times of recession.

HEINEMANN ADVANCED HISTORY

In addition, the process of European integration began in 1950–1 with **the Schuman Plan** and the formation of the European Coal and Steel Community. Britain's relationships with Europe were complicated by its links with the empire and Commonwealth, such as extensive trade with New Zealand. Also the whole period was dominated by the Cold War, both by the division of Europe and by extensive US economic involvement in Europe.

Finally, although successive governments continued the so-called post-war consensus, British politics, with its first-past-the-post electoral system, frequently accentuated sharp differences in ideology and economic policy (and on industrial relations and the role of the unions). This was unlike Germany, for example, where there were coalition governments and considerable consistency in economic policy regardless of which party was in power.

Timeline of the British economy, 1951–97

Within this framework, it is possible to set out the arguments for two contrasting views of British economic performance.

> *A 'Golden Age', 1951–73?*
> 1951   The end of the second Attlee government and the start of thirteen years of Conservative dominance.
> 1959   Macmillan's election victory: 'You've never had it so good.'
> 1964   Labour in power under Harold Wilson, with ambitious plans for economic modernisation.
> 1970   Conservatives back in power under Edward Heath.
> 1973   British entry into the EEC after previous failed applications in 1961 and 1967.
>
> *The oil-price crisis and its consequences*
> 1974   The three-day week and the fall of Heath's government.
> 1976   High inflation and Britain's application for an IMF loan.
> 1979   Defeat of the Callaghan government after the 'Winter of Discontent'.
>
> *A 'Thatcher Revolution', 1979–97?*
> 1981   The impact of 'monetarist' policies on industry.
> 1984   Industrial conflict and the miners' strike.
> 1987   The 'Big Bang' and financial deregulation.
> 1990   The fall of Margaret Thatcher.
> 1992   'Black Wednesday' and Britain's exit from the ERM.
> 1997   Labour's election victory and the end of eighteen years of Conservative rule.

KEY EVENT

The Schuman Plan 1950 established the Coal and Steel Community. This set up close integration of French and German heavy industry and laid the foundations for the future EEC.

THE NEGATIVE VIEW: CONTINUOUS ECONOMIC DECLINE?
Factors causing lost opportunities, 1951–73

- **Over-ambitious spending policies.** After the war, British governments attempted to maintain a costly world role at the same time as nationalising key industries and bringing in the Welfare State. In 1951, the impact of the Korean War and the split between Bevan and Gaitskell (see page 50) revealed that the economy was under strain.

- **Failure to invest and restructure after the war.** In *The Lost Victory* (1995), Correlli Barnett claims that the British economy continued to rely on a **Victorian structure**. Macmillan, Wilson and Heath all began their premierships with urgent plans for economic modernisation; looking back all three felt that they had failed to achieve significant success.

- **Failure to succeed in the drive for exports.** Between 1950 and 1970, Britain's share of world trade declined from a quarter to ten per cent. In shipbuilding, the tonnage produced by British shipyards collapsed from 37 per cent to less than four per cent. The British car industry had a dominant position in the 1950s but volume car production ran into difficulties from the 1960s, with the rise of imports from Europe and Japan.

- **Low productivity.** The number of person-hours required for manufactured products was significantly higher in Britain than for foreign competitors.

- **Excessive government intervention.** It has been argued that this protected inefficient industries from the rigours of competition and burdened efficient industries with high taxes and over-regulation.

- **The weaknesses of technological education.** Britain's education system has been accused of an undue bias towards the arts and humanities and a lack of status for science and technology. For example, Germany was far more likely to have graduate production managers than Britain.

- **Lower growth rates than foreign competitors.** See the table below.

KEY FACT

Victorian structure
Barnett claimed that British industry did not modernise after the war, either in plant and machinery or in management methods.

KEY TERM

Gross Domestic Product (GDP) a term used by economists to assess the total 'value' of the national economy.

Relative growth rates 1950–73 (percentage annual growth).

	UK	USA	West Germany	Japan
Gross Domestic Product	3.0	3.7	5.9	9.4
Real GDP per head	2.9	2.1	4.7	7.8
Real GDP per hours worked	3.1	2.4	5.7	7.4

'Stop–Go' economy. Above all, the economy in this period ran on the cycle of 'Stop–Go'. From the 1950s onwards, bursts of economic growth and consumer spending ('Go') were halted by fears of inflation and recurrent balance of payments crises, leading to government action to cut demand and thus to increased unemployment ('Stop'). This was a particular difficulty for the Conservatives under Macmillan, with sharp slow-downs in 1958 and 1962. Economic considerations were the main reason why Macmillan was converted to the view that Britain should apply for membership of the EEC in 1961; when de Gaulle vetoed Britain's application in 1963, it was a big economic setback.

The Labour government had ambitious plans to restructure the economy in what Harold Wilson termed the 'white heat of the technological revolution'. However, these plans collapsed in 1967 with the devaluation of the pound and with gaping divisions within the Labour Cabinet, where George Brown's new Department of Economic Affairs clashed with the Treasury. Wilson also attempted large-scale reform of trade union power through his White Paper 'In Place of Strife'; but then backed away from confrontation with the unions, leaving unsolved problems to fester. Despite the prosperity levels of the 1960s, it can be argued that the underlying weaknesses of the British economy were never really tackled.

The crisis of the 1970s

When the long post-war boom ended in 1973, short-term pressures after the oil price crisis combined with deeper structural weaknesses to produce a major depression and much gloom about the prospects for the economy.

There was a damaging miners' strike in 1973–4 that did much to persuade Edward Heath's government to introduce the three-day week and then to call a general election in 1974. After Labour returned to power, both Wilson's and Callaghan's governments found massive difficulties in overcoming industrial unrest, or in avoiding splits within the Labour Party about how to deal with it.

The government was also faced with rising unemployment and financial instability. In addition to rising unemployment, this was a period of rapid inflation. In 1976, the pound lost almost a quarter of its value against the US dollar. The Chancellor, Denis Healey, was forced to take out a massive loan from the International Monetary Fund. This was a humiliating admission of weakness. The loan could be gained only on the condition that there were large cuts in government spending, which inevitably made the splits in the Labour Party worse.

KEY TERM

Monetarist policies involved restricting government debt and leaving struggling industries to sink or swim. As a result there was a sharp rise in unemployment between 1979 and 1981.

KEY TERM

The International Monetary Fund (IMF) was set up in 1944 at the Bretton Woods conference. In 1976, Britain was forced to apply for a large IMF loan to deal with the financial crisis.

Failures during the 1980s and 1990s

There was a significant decline in manufacturing during this period. The **monetarist policies** of the Thatcher government from 1979, intended to cure the 'British disease', initially made the decline of industry worse. Two million jobs in manufacturing were lost and exports declined.

There were also continued problems in industrial relations. The miners' strike of 1984–5 was the most famous of a number of disputes. In addition, there was widespread demoralisation in the public sector and failure to invest the profits of privatisations.

THE POSITIVE VIEW: SUSTAINED ECONOMIC SUCCESS?
Factors in the post-war boom, c.1950–73

There was stability of the international monetary system. The Bretton Woods Conference of July 1944 established **The International Monetary Fund (IMF)** and, together with the permanent dominance of the US dollar, led to international stability very different from that of the interwar years. The initiation of the General Agreement on Tariffs and Trade (GATT) in 1947 also helped to reduce trade barriers and encourage growth. Between 1951 and 1973, the average annual rate of growth of GDP was 2.8 per cent. This was far better than long-term growth rates in the interwar years, or in the period before the First World War. In addition to this sustained economic growth there was low unemployment and relatively low inflation. The average annual rate of unemployment was two per cent; in the 1930s, the equivalent annual average was 12.7 per cent. Even in the 1970s recession, unemployment was rarely above one million; in the interwar years, unemployment was never less than one million. During this period living standards were rising. Infant mortality halved between 1950 and 1973. Weekly earnings rose, hours worked fell. Car ownership increased from 46 cars per thousand to 247 cars per thousand. By 1973, two-thirds of households had washing machines and refrigerators; in 1950, it had been five per cent. By 1973, one household in five possessed a colour TV set.

During this period, both Labour and Conservative governments were successful in maintaining stable exchange rates and in ensuring that the 'Stop-Go' cycle actually produced a mostly prosperous and stable outcome overall. The Macmillan government was especially successful in recovering from the downturn of 1958; the Labour government, through Roy Jenkins, recovered extremely well by 1970 from the devaluation crisis of 1967.

Factors in the recovery from crisis, 1973–97

In the period 1973–97 there were improvements in trade. British entry to the EEC in 1973 reflected an appreciation that British trade links with Europe were much more significant than the traditional ties with the Commonwealth countries. Between 1973 and 1993, the proportion of British trade with Common Market partners rose from about 30 per cent to more than 50 per cent. It was also during this period that Britain became a net exporter of North Sea oil, which hugely strengthened the balance of payments. Firmer government policies against trade union power were introduced. Both Edward Heath and James Callaghan had recognised the need for restraints on pay and on the bargaining power of the trade unions. In the 1980s, Mrs Thatcher succeeded in driving through controversial policies curbing union power. This was a painful transition and may well have been unnecessarily divisive, but most observers agree that it was a vital factor in increasing competitiveness. There was an end to subsidies to inefficient enterprises. Edward Heath had set out in 1970 with the intention of making industries stand on their own feet, but had been undermined by the impact of the oil price crisis. The Callaghan government also tried to move in this direction after 1976 but Callaghan did not have a big enough majority, or enough political will, to carry the policy through. Mrs Thatcher had both the will and the working majority and, as a result, Britain became much more competitive, which helped a rise in productivity (see table below).

	1973–9	1980–90
UK	0.6	1.5
West Germany	1.8	0.8
France	1.7	1.7
USA	-0.4	0.5
Japan	1.4	2.0

Productivity growth in the major industrial economies, 1973–90.

The 1980s was indeed a period of painful restructuring and the drastic slimming down of traditional industries. There were 170,000 men employed in coalmining in the early 1970s; by the mid-1990s, that number had shrunk to about 30,000. The positive view of Britain's economic performance is based on the assumption that this restructuring was successfully completed. From the depths of the crisis years up to 1981, there was a burst of prosperity during the 'Lawson boom' of the 1980s see page 100. From the recession of the early 1990s and the crisis

KEY PEOPLE

Gordon Brown
(1951-) Scottish Labour politician, who was shadow chancellor from 1992-97 and Chancellor from 1997. The alliance between Brown and Blair was a key factor in the rise of 'New Labour' from 1994, when Brown agreed to stand aside to give Blair a free run to succeed John Smith.

Tony Blair
(1953-) succeeded John Smith as Labour leader in 1994. Together with Gordon Brown, he was instrumental in the modernisation of the Labour Party, both in presentation and in developing centrist policies to appeal to 'Middle England'. Became Prime Minister after the Labour landslide of 1997.

over the ERM, there was another sustained boom in the Major years. Many observers, not only Conservative politicians, claim that Labour inherited a healthy economic situation in 1997, which was the foundation of the successes of the new Labour Chancellor, **Gordon Brown**.

CONCLUSIONS

As noted at the start of this section, it is extremely difficult to resolve the debate about Britain's post-war economic performance. This difficulty is neatly represented by the differing interpretations of Labour's election victory in 1997. It might seem that the lesson of this Labour landslide was obvious: that the electorate had rejected eighteen years of Conservatism in general and Thatcherism in particular and was ready for a return to more left-of-centre policies. However, this interpretation is not so obvious. Several observers, including many on the left wing of the Labour Party, would assert that 1997 marked not the rejection of Thatcher's legacy but its continuation under **Tony Blair**. As usual, one historian's turning point is another historian's time of continuity.

Any evaluation of Britain's economic situation by 1997 compared with that at the end of the Second World War has to recognise the extent of progress in terms of living standards and the consumer economy. In the late 1990s, the British people as a whole had greater spending power, were better dressed and better housed. Rationing was a distant memory for the older generation. So was war itself: Britain and Europe during the Cold War era enjoyed greater peace and stability than was ever the case before, or seems likely to be the case in the uncertain post-Cold War future. Was this progress sufficient to justify claims of sustained economic success? Or was it indeed a time when British governments did no more than manage decline?

The following three alternative interpretations are by no means the only ones possible, but they provide a basis for reaching a judgement.

The Thatcherite view

Britain followed the wrong economic path from 1951–79. 'Butskellism' was a mistake; there were too many nationalisations, too little investment and competition, too much spending on the Welfare State, too little focus on modern management techniques, too much government intervention by the 'nanny state'. These policies led to the disasters of the 'Winter of Discontent'. The period after 1979 was a revival. Monetarism replaced socialism; the unions were tamed. The public sector and especially the civil service came under the discipline of market forces and Britain became competitive. This was recognised even by Thatcher's opponents who did little in and after 1997 to alter the broad direction of the free-market economy.

The view from the 'Golden Age'

The post-war boom was a period of sustained social and economic success. Between 1951 and 1973, Britain became a more prosperous and equal society, recovering admirably well from the war and from the difficult interwar years. After the crisis of the 1970s, the Thatcher government took an unnecessary axe to the post-war consensus and carried through policies that were socially divisive and did terrible damage to manufacturing industry. This was recognised when Thatcher's own party rejected her and the new government under John Major turned away from her extreme approach.

The 'balanced' view

(Note that the balanced view is not automatically the right one!)

The post-war recovery was a relative success but also a relative failure in terms of investment and competitiveness. After 1979, Thatcher's economic reforms were necessary and in some ways successfully completed but at too high a price in social divisions. In any case, it can be argued that Thatcher's policies were much less ideological than is sometimes supposed: Thatcher made many compromises with the old ways of 'Stop–Go'. Britain's economy coped well with two major depressions in the 1970s and at the end of the 1980s. The period between 1951 and 1997 has been uneven but broadly a relatively successful part of the post-war prosperity of Western Europe as a whole.

SECTION 5

Was there a 'Thatcher Revolution' between 1979 and 1990?

ASSESSING THATCHER: THE CONTROVERSY

Few, if any, British prime ministers have aroused such intense and lasting controversies as Margaret Thatcher. Between 1979 and 1990, her radical policies and her combative style of government polarised political and public opinion. The manner of her fall caused bitter divisions within her party and considerable celebrations among her enemies.

Broadly, there are three alternative interpretations of the Thatcher legacy.

- There was a 'Thatcher Revolution' and it was beneficial. She smashed the cosy, complacent post-war consensus and rescued Britain from slow, irreversible decline.
- There was a 'Thatcher Revolution' and it did lasting harm to Britain. It created unnecessary damage to British manufacturing industry; it led to the triumph of private greed over the public good, and it was socially and politically divisive.
- There was no 'Thatcher Revolution' at all. Thatcher was unable to complete the transformation she had aimed for; the old ways of British

Margaret
Thatcher as
prime minister
1987.

government and politics (and the Conservative Party) resisted her attempts at fundamental reform.

These interpretations concern relatively recent history; it is not yet possible for historians to take the long view. Much of the debate about Thatcher and Thatcherism remains highly subjective and partisan, and often very personalised, either in denunciation or approval. Nevertheless, it is important to attempt a balanced judgement of the Thatcher years and whether they constituted a 'revolution' for either the country or the Conservative Party or both.

It is also important to recognise change over time. Thatcher's personal style and approach to cabinet government was very different by 1990 than when she first came to power in 1979. Her three election victories provide a convenient guide to her time in office. From 1979–83 she established her position as leader after arriving in power as an unknown quantity, experienced a major economic and social crisis and recovered with the help of victory in the Falklands War to win a decisive victory. 1983–87 were years of almost total dominance when she defeated the miners, established a close relationship with the **Reagan** administration, became one of the significant leaders of the European Community, and appeared close to invincible at her third election victory in 1987. From 1987 onwards she began to become more isolated, both in Europe and in relations with her own Cabinet, she faced a sharp decline in her standing in the opinion polls before her surprising rejection by her own party in 1990.

Whether these changes over time, and her fall in 1990, represented political failure on her part or 'betrayal' by an ungrateful party, is a matter for debate. A summary of Mrs Thatcher's achievements provides a basis for assessment and evaluation. In basic terms these include the sale of council houses, privatisation of state enterprises, reform of the civil service, curbing of the unions and forcing the Labour Party to abandon its socialist traditions. Were these aims carried through? Did they lead to significant and lasting change? Was Mrs Thatcher responsible for them?

WHAT WAS THE STATE OF BRITISH SOCIETY AND POLITICS IN 1979?

The circumstances in which Margaret Thatcher came to power in 1979 were exceptional and the future direction for Britain was very uncertain. After the long post-war boom ended with the oil price crisis of 1973 (see Section 4, page 76), the economic situation was very difficult. There had been years of rising inflation and a sharp decline in manufacturing output. Industrial relations were extremely bad, symbolised by the

KEY PERSON

Ronald Reagan (1911–) Reagan was elected President in 1980. A conservative Republican he was keen to take a strong line in the Cold War. He and Mrs Thatcher worked closely together in dealing with the USSR, especially after Mikhail Gorbachev came to power in 1985 (see page 119).

'Winter of Discontent' that had done so much to bring down the Callaghan government. The crisis in Northern Ireland appeared impossible to solve (see Section 5, pages 137–149). Many observers regarded Britain as facing not a passing phase but a deep structural crisis. If this was indeed the case, then the impact of Mrs Thatcher after 1979 was crucial.

Against this, it has been claimed by many historians that the economic crisis of the late 1970s marked merely a temporary blip in the long-term post-war prosperity and success of Britain (and Western Europe as a whole). In their view, there would eventually have been a natural economic recovery in the 1980s; it was not necessary to adopt drastic policies to achieve this (pages 104–112). Moreover, if the post-war consensus was overall a good thing, then it did not need to be smashed in order to make way for Thatcherism. Any evaluation of the achievements of the Thatcher era must start with an assessment of how desperate, or not, the condition of Britain was in 1979.

KEY PERSON

Michael Heseltine
(1933–) a millionaire publisher and charismatic politician who became an MP in 1966. He played a big part in assisting inner cities after the riots of the 1980s. He resigned from the cabinet in 1986 over the Westland Affair. His leadership challenge in 1990 brought Mrs Thatcher down.

HOW RADICAL WERE THATCHER'S AIMS AND POLICIES?

It was not only the Labour Party that was at a political crossroads in 1979; Margaret Thatcher had won the leadership of the Conservative Party in 1975 as a rebel against the so-called 'corporatism' of Edward Heath's government. (The long-running feud between Thatcher and Heath after 1979 was indeed based on a clash of personalities; but it was also based on deep political and ideological differences about the direction the Conservative Party should follow (as was her feud with **Michael Heseltine**).) Thatcher offered a new kind of Conservatism. She intended to shake up her own party just as radically as she intended to shake up the country as a whole.

'Thatcherism' can be defined in various ways, there was a strong emphasis on personal leadership, on dynamic and decisive action, which ignored the politics of consensus. It had a sharply anti-socialist ideology, strongly opposed to socialism at home and to Soviet communism abroad. There was emphasis on the personal responsibilities of the citizen, moving away from the 'nanny state' and the culture of dependence. The economic philosophy, was strongly influenced by the ideas of 'monetarism' and by determination to reduce economic interventions by the state. Thatcherism had a drive towards greater industrial competitiveness, privatisation and probable confrontations with the unions. Foreign policy was more assertive and intensified the Cold War. And finally there was a wider involvement of ordinary people in the capitalist economy, through self-help, shares and savings, and home ownership.

The drive towards radical change in the British economy and in the Conservative Party was built into the circumstances in which Mrs Thatcher gained the leadership in 1975. What happened in 1975 was a *coup d'état* against Edward Heath. The key economic ideas from **Keith Joseph** were an attack on the previous direction of Conservative policy, especially towards state industrial concerns and the trade unions. The guiding idea was that Keyensian economic thinking had been dominant for too long and that the **ideas of monetarism**, as set out by Friedrich Hayek and Milton Friedman, should be followed in future. As leader of the opposition and during the election campaign in 1979, Mrs Thatcher made it plain that she was a conviction politician, determined to take a radical approach to the economy.

Taken at face value, the ideals of Thatcherism do indeed suggest a revolutionary break with the past. Many historians, both those who admired Thatcher and those who hated everything she stood for, remain convinced that 1979 was a landmark year, marking the end of the Attlee post-war consensus and 'Butskellism', and the beginning of a 'Thatcher Revolution'.

On the other hand, it can be argued that Thatcher was a much more cautious and pragmatic politician than the image of the **'Iron Lady'** suggests. Thatcher depended in the early years on a number of highly traditional Conservative ministers, such as the conciliatory Willie Whitelaw. She avoided risks and made many compromises. Despite her many public Eurosceptic pronouncements since losing power in 1990, Thatcherism in 1979 was certainly far from being openly anti-European. Indeed, Thatcher's government took many actions which led to closer European integration. The radicalism of Margaret Thatcher may have been less to do with the substance of policies and more to do with her style of leadership and rhetoric.

IN WHAT WAYS WAS THATCHERISM POPULAR?

Measuring the popularity of Margaret Thatcher's political agenda is difficult. Many supported her policies without much enthusiasm for the woman herself. Attitudes towards her changed over time. Above all, there was the problem of the virtually non-existent opposition. Many claim that Thatcher came to power not because of a pro-Thatcher mood but largely as the result of the failures of the Labour governments of Wilson and Callaghan at a time of dire economic crisis. Thatcher's position was then strengthened in the early 1980s by the fact that Labour was made unelectable by the antics of the Left and by the breaking away of the SDP.

Even with the divisions among those who opposed the Conservatives, Margaret Thatcher was deeply unpopular by 1981 and opinion polls were

Keith Joseph (1918-1994) was an influential theorist who provided the right wing of the Conservative Party with new policy ideas in the 1970s. He helped Mrs Thatcher to displace Edward Heath in 1975. He was education secretary from 1981 to 1986.

Ideas of monetarism were associated with Friedrich Hayek and the 'Chicago school' of economists. Monetarism argued against state support for struggling industries, and was a swing away from the Keynesian ideas which had influenced economic thinking in the post-war years.

Iron Lady was a term of abuse aimed at Mrs Thatcher's doctrinaire approach to politics but she actually liked the description and often used it about herself.

predicting doom for the Conservatives and stunning successes for the Liberals and the SDP; until, that is, Thatcher was 'saved' by the Falklands War just in time for the 1983 election. It was also true that Thatcher did not notably increase the total Conservative vote; her massive majorities in 1983 and 1987 were due to the collapse of the Labour vote, not any surge in support for the Conservatives.

Thatcher's election victories.

| Year | Seats and share of the popular vote | | | |
	Conservative	Labour	Liberal & SDP	Others
1979	339 (44%)	268 (37%)	11 (14%)	16 (5%)
1983	397 (42%)	209 (28%)	23 (25%)	21 (5%)
1987	375 (42%)	229 (31%)	22 (23%)	24 (4%)

WHAT WERE THATCHER'S POLICIES AND ACHIEVEMENTS IN POWER?
The first term, 1979–83

In the 1979 election, Margaret Thatcher had overcome her image as stridently right wing and unelectable; she was skilful in moving towards the middle ground and was especially effective in appealing to skilled workers. However, her economic policies were based on a rigid application of monetarism, the immediate consequences of which were a very painful recession in 1979–82:

- unemployment rose from 1.2 million to 3 million
- industrial output fell by an average of eleven per cent
- interest rates rose to just under sixteen per cent
- the pound rose to a value against the US dollar of $2.45; this had a ruinous impact on export-based industries such as engineering
- there was a marked split between North and South: northern areas took the brunt of industrial closures; the services sector in the South fared much better
- there was unrest and social tensions, with major rioting in depressed urban areas such as St Paul's in Bristol and Toxteth in Liverpool in 1981.

Thatcher was massively unpopular by the end of 1981 but was able to recover from economic crisis and win the 1983 general election because of a number of successes and favourable factors. These included a slight economic recovery in 1982 – inflation and interest rates fell and the economy began to benefit from North Sea oil. There was also a surge in Thatcher's popularity after victory in the Falklands War. This coincided with a weakening of Labour as the main Party of Opposition: the emergence of the breakaway SDP split the Labour vote and the perception of weak leadership by **Michael Foot** compared badly with Thatcher's self-confidence and certainty. Thatcher was also helped by the unrealistic policies dictated by the **Bennite Left** and which influenced the Labour Party's 1983 election manifesto, known as the 'longest suicide note in history'.

The second term, 1983–7

Thatcher was vastly strengthened by victory in 1983. She had increased her majority to 144 seats and had a psychological dominance over the opposition parties. She also gained control more over the Conservative Party, having removed or marginalised many of the traditional 'One Nation' Tories who had been reluctant to follow her radical policies in a cabinet reshuffle of 1981. Thatcher was now in a position to pursue her main objectives:

- to cut inflation (the curse of the 1970s) to as near zero as possible
- to cut public spending, especially by cutting back on local government, and to 'roll back the state' by privatisation of nationalised industries
- to cut taxes, especially income tax
- to deregulate the economy and the financial system
- to reform the civil service and make it less obstructive to government policy
- to curb trade union power.

There were several successes. The sale of council houses was popular. State-controlled industries such as British Gas, British Airways and British Leyland were privatised. Laws were introduced against secondary picketing (workers on strike in one industry try to persuade workers in another industry to join) and the government won a bitter struggle against trade union opposition, especially over the print unions and the long-running miners' strike in 1984–5. Local government finances were virtually centralised under the control of the Treasury and the expanded Department of the Environment; the symbol of Thatcher's war against local government was the abolition of the Greater London Council. The financial markets were deregulated by the 'Big Bang' (the deregulation of stock market and financial services) in 1987. There was a consumer boom, partly because of easy credit and rising house prices, and partly because of 'windfalls' from privatisations.

Thatcher had also gained huge personal prestige by the mid-1980s, for example by her unblinking bravery when the IRA blew up her hotel in **Brighton** during the Conservative Party conference in October 1984. She was rather pleased to be known as the Iron Lady and to be a prominent ally of President Reagan at a time when the 'New Cold War' was intensifying.

KEY PERSON

Michael Foot (1913-) was a left-wing journalist (one of the authors of the 'Guilty Men' pamphlet in 1940) and a loyal supporter of Nye Bevan. He became an MP in 1945 but had no experience in government until 1974. When Jim Callaghan resigned, Foot surprisingly became party leader in preference to Denis Healey. He led an ineffectual election campaign in 1983 and resigned after Labour's heavy defeat.

KEY TERM

Bennite Left emerged in Labour's years of opposition after 1979 and had great success in imposing left-wing policies on the party. But the influence of the Left declined after Neil Kinnock became leader in 1983 and virtually disappeared in the 1990s with the rise of 'New Labour'.

Her successes were not complete. Thatcherism failed to make much headway with cutting government expenditure. There was little or no industrial recovery and the problems of the older industrialised regions remained severe. The taming of the trade unions came at a high price in hardship and social divisions; the tendency of Thatcher to refer to her opponents as 'the enemy within' made these divisions worse. The profits from North Sea oil and from selling off state concerns were not invested in major projects for economic modernisation but went to fuel the consumer boom.

The final years, 1987–90

After the 1987 election, Margaret Thatcher appeared unstoppable. By this time, Mikhail Gorbachev had emerged as the reformist leader of the Soviet Union and Thatcher had established a surprisingly successful working relationship with him. When the Berlin Wall came down in November 1989, it appeared as if Thatcher's hard-line policies had helped to win the Cold War. She had achieved an enormous reputation abroad. At home, however, her final years in office were marked by growing difficulties; above all, Thatcher became very isolated within her own party. She had established a close circle of favoured advisers, such as **Bernard Ingham** and **Charles Powell**, but had lost several important people, notably by the death of Willie Whitelaw and by the resignation of Cecil Parkinson after a personal scandal. Already, in 1986, the resignation of Michael Heseltine over **the Westland Affair** was a sign of dangerous difficulties with her Cabinet.

Between 1988 and 1990, Mrs Thatcher lost the confidence and support of key members of her government. This was mostly due to two key factors. One was the issue of Europe (see pages 100–101) where her growing reluctance to carry through the logical results of the policies she had followed earlier in the 1980s alienated pro-European ministers such as Geoffrey Howe. The second was her tendency towards an authoritarian approach, showing less and less patience with alternative views. The Chancellor Nigel Lawson resigned in 1988; Geoffrey Howe was sacked as Foreign Secretary; even the ultra-loyalist Thatcherite Norman Tebbit was moving away from her inner circle. Thatcher insisted pushing through her most controversial measure of all, **the poll tax**, despite all of the warnings from her Cabinet.

By 1990, the opinion polls were showing a disastrous decline in support for the Conservatives, partly because there was at last a credible Labour opposition for the first time since Thatcher's 1979 election victory. The result was a leadership challenge from Michael Heseltine and a highly damaging attack in Parliament from Geoffrey Howe. Thatcher's position within the Party proved to be surprisingly vulnerable. Having only narrowly won the first round of the leadership election, she looked for support from her Cabinet and did not find any. Her fall was a huge public surprise but, like Churchill's defeat in 1945, perhaps it should not have been.

'Tell Mrs Thatcher we've changed our minds — we think the poll tax sounds an absolutely splendid idea'

A Matthew Pritchard political cartoon showing anti-Thatcher/ anti-Poll Tax feeling among the cabinet in 1988.

HOW FAR DID THATCHER CHANGE THE CONSERVATIVE PARTY?

After 1990, the lasting effects of Thatcherism upon the Conservative Party remain contentious. Her admirers pointed to three consecutive election victories and the longest period in power of any prime minister since Lord Liverpool at the beginning of the nineteenth century. Her detractors pointed to the fact that the Conservative Party of the 1990s was split beyond repair, with an ageing and declining membership, it suffered catastrophic defeats in 1997 and 2001. Even the circumstances of Thatcher's removal from the leadership in 1990 are disputed. Thatcher supporters claim that this 'regicide' was a shameful and ungrateful act, with disastrous consequences for the Party. Her opponents claim that in 1990 the Conservative Party was headed for certain defeat under an increasingly unpopular leader and her even more unpopular poll tax; that her removal came just in time to enable the Party to win the 1992 election under John Major.

John Major himself represented a puzzle in terms of the legacy of Thatcherism. Backing from Thatcher and her supporters was a vital factor in bringing Major to the leadership; he was seen as the ideal candidate to block the chances of the hated Michael Heseltine. However, Major's style in office proved to be mostly centrist and conciliatory, often appealing to traditional Conservative values. Thatcherites soon became some of Major's bitterest opponents .

The 'European question'

The issue of Europe made the true importance of Thatcher's legacy even more complex. It is possible that the apparently insoluble divisions within the Party are fundamentally not about Thatcherism but about Europe – that the personality and politics of the leader could not make much difference unless and until the question of Europe is somehow settled once and for all. It is equally possible that it was not Europe that fatally divided the Party, but Mrs Thatcher herself. One large section of the Conservative Party was indeed radically altered by Thatcher's personality and politics, and by the influx of a new wave of Thatcherite MPs, while a significant section of the Party remained in the traditions of Harold Macmillan and Edward Heath. For many experienced observers of the political scene, the impact of Margaret Thatcher did more to change (and in the long run to benefit) the Labour Party than the Conservatives.

HOW FUNDAMENTALLY DIFFERENT HAD BRITAIN BECOME BY THE EARLY 1990S?

Society and politics in Britain undeniably experienced significant changes during the Thatcher era. An assessment of whether these changes amounted to a 'Thatcher Revolution' or not has been argued in different ways by different historians. It is striking, however, that it was not only admirers of Thatcher who claimed that she brought about fundamental change. In 2002, the Marxist historian Eric Hobsbawm wrote in his memoirs, *Interesting Times*:

The Thatcher era was the nearest thing in the twentieth century to a political, social and cultural revolution – and not one for the better. It was directed against the traditional ruling classes and the country's established institutions, and against the Labour movement. In the course of this largely successful endeavour, it obliterated most of the traditional British values and made the country unrecognisable.

Hobsbawm was just about as hostile to Thatcher and all her works as it was possible to be and yet he had no doubts that she had changed Britain fundamentally. Several historians and political commentators have agreed with Hobsbawm on this issue but have regarded the results of the 'Thatcher Revolution' in a positive light, such as the Thatcher loyalist Norman Tebbit writing in 1988:

In the last eight years, there has been a revolution whose chief casualties have been socialism and the weak complacent Conservatism of the 1960s and early 1970s. The 'Thatcher Revolution' has come a long way but most of its work so far has been devoted to the destruction of the restraints which had brought our economy to its knees. The task for the next stage must be rebuilding the social restraints which have been greatly weakened by the doctrines of the permissive society.

It is interesting to note that even Tebbit thought that the 'Thatcher Revolution' was unfinished. Some historians have claimed that it remained unfinished to the end and was even thrown into reverse, as in the view put forward in 1992 by Ken Morgan:

The Thatcher years came to an end not through electoral defeat but through a grass-roots movement within the Conservative Party. It reflected a wider national mood. The basic logic of her programme since 1979 had been to reverse the main lines of her country's history since 1945. Through ceaseless activity and a triumph of will power, she came near to success; but below the surface, the nation had defeated her.

Why was there such a dramatic Conservative decline and Labour recovery in the 1990s?

At the high tide of Thatcherism on election night in 1987, the Conservative domination of British politics seemed more complete than at any other time in modern history. Mrs Thatcher had achieved almost legendary status at home and abroad. The Conservative electoral machine was as slick and efficient as ever. Yet another heavy election defeat seemed to indicate that the Labour opposition was in permanent decline. This impression of the 'death of socialism' was underlined in 1989 by revolutions that brought the end of the Berlin Wall and the collapse of the Soviet Empire in Eastern Europe. The notion that, within ten years, the Conservatives would be in disarray and Labour would be poised for an even bigger election miracle than the 1945 landslide, was unthinkable. Yet it happened.

To explain the spectacular success of New Labour by 1997 requires a synoptic view of political developments in the 1980s and the 1990s, involving at least four elements:

- causes of Conservative decline under John Major from 1992
- analysis of underlying weaknesses beneath the surface of Conservative dominance in the 1980s
- causes of Labour's success under Tony Blair from 1994
- analysis of long-term factors already pointing towards Labour recovery between 1983 and 1994.

Resolving these issues involves other significant questions.

- How close did the SDP and the Liberals come in the 1980s to breaking the mould of the two-party system?
- Was the success of New Labour a continuation or a rejection of the 'socialist' past of the Labour Party?
- Was the decline of the Conservatives caused by Thatcherism or caused by the Party's rejection of Thatcher?

WHY WAS LABOUR SO UNSUCCESSFUL IN THE 1980S?
The end of the Callaghan government in 1979 was a dramatic turning point for both of the main political parties. Callaghan, and perhaps even more so Harold Wilson, had presided over a party that was deeply divided on a number of key political issues. In government, it had been

possible, just, to keep the lid on the internal pressures in the Labour movement, but being in opposition brought these deep and widening differences into the open.

1978–9	The 'Winter of Discontent'.
1979	Thatcher's victory in the general election; Michael Foot elected leader of the Labour Party.
1980	Bitter disputes at the Labour Party conference in Blackpool.
1981	The formation of the Social Democratic Party (SDP) by the 'Gang of Four'.
1983	Disastrous defeat in the general election; Neil Kinnock elected Labour Party leader.
1984	Adverse publicity about 'Militant', especially in Liverpool.
1984–5	The miners' strike.
1987	Thatcher's third general election victory.

The decline of the Labour Party, 1979–87.

Shirley Williams (1930-) right wing of the Labour Party and a strong supporter of the ideas of Anthony Crosland. After the 1979 election she became a target for attacks from the Bennite Left. She was one of the 'Gang of Four' and was President of the SDP from 1982 until it merged with the Liberals.

David Owen (1938-) disillusioned by Labour's shift to the left he became leader of the SDP from 1981.

Why was the Labour Party so weak and divided by 1983?

There were differences in ideology that were reflected in the rise of the Bennite Left and by the resurgence of the campaign against nuclear armaments. The 1980s was the decade of cruise missiles and the close relationship between Margaret Thatcher and Ronald Reagan. Many groups, such as the Greenham Women campaigning against cruise missiles, became involved in single-issue politics and were diverted away from what might in other circumstances have been support for the Labour Party. Personality clashes caused a divisive campaign to succeed Callaghan, which ultimately led to the defeat of Denis Healey by Michael Foot. Significant differences over Europe existed, in the 1975 EEC Referendum, for example, Tony Benn had campaigned energetically against the whole idea of British engagement with Europe, while Roy Jenkins and Denis Healey were equally enthusiastically in favour. After 1979, divisions about Europe became fiercer as the Left felt it was gaining the upper hand. The Social Democratic Party emerged. This completely new political party was based on the breakaway Labour MPs Roy Jenkins, **Shirley Williams**, **David Owen** and Bill Rodgers. The SDP attracted support from important sections of previous Labour supporters and seriously damaged Labour's electoral chances. In the 1983 election, the SDP in alliance with the Liberals took a large share of the 'anti-Thatcher vote' (see page 117). There was a growing split between the trade unions and the Labour Party. This was made much worse by a series of high-profile industrial disputes, especially those involving the print unions

Why was there such a dramatic Conservative decline and Labour recovery in the 1990s?

and the National Union of Mineworkers led by **Arthur Scargill**. The fundamental problem of how the Labour Party should adapt to social and economic change was a major cause of weakness and division. At precisely the time that the left wing of the Labour Party was becoming more militant and more enthusiastic about class war, the economic basis of the party (mass unionised labour in manufacturing industries) was disappearing. The working classes were going through massive sociological changes due to new technologies, for example in the mechanisation of car manufacturing, the containerisation of shipping and the ever increasing use of computers. There was also, the special problem posed by Margaret Thatcher. She not only threatened to turn her own Party upside down, she had a massive impact on the Labour party, too, not least because her appeal reached many former Labour voters such as skilled workers anxious to protect earnings differentials, those impressed by Thatcher's resolute approach to the Falklands War, traditionalists offended by the extreme antics of the Bennites, or the Scargillites, or militant left-wing councils, and former Labour voters satisfied by the sale of council houses.

What was the significance of the SDP?

The Social Democrat Party was, and remains, a very controversial subject for the Labour Party. The 'Gang of Four' included well-known, popular and highly experienced politicians. Roy Jenkins had been Deputy Leader and one of the best Chancellors Labour ever had. David Owen was one of the brightest stars in the Callaghan Cabinet, seen by some as a possible future leader. Shirley Williams was a particularly painful loss: she was a well-liked moderate who represented a strand of voters Labour had to win over to stand any chance of electoral success. She had left the Party because she had been hounded out of it by the Left, not because she wanted to leave or because of any personal ambitions.

To many observers, the establishment of the SDP was ultimately of great benefit to Labour: it is argued that the SDP breakaway forced the Party back to sanity by bringing out into the open the realisation of how unelectable Labour had become. Thus, the theory goes, the SDP 'saved' the Labour Party by leaving it, though such an analysis is sharply rejected by Labour loyalists. The Labour Party had never forgotten how it had been scarred by Ramsay MacDonald's 'betrayal' in 1931; the accusation came easily that the SDP was another such betrayal. It is significant that who liked and admired the SDP rebels were bitterly critical of them for not remaining in the Party to carry on the fight. Whether the effect of the SDP was more important for weakening and dividing the Party in the short term, or for enabling its eventual Blairite recovery in the long term, remains a very open question.

KEY PEOPLE

Arthur Scargill(1938-) militant leader of the NUM (National Union of Mineworkers). Scargill had led successful strikes in 1972 and 1974. He played the key role in the Miners' strike of 1984-85, believing in mass picketing and political confrontation with government. After the defeat of the strike, NUM membership declined. In the 1990s, Scargill was hostile to Tony Blair and 'New Labour'.

Neil Kinnock(1942-)
Welsh Labour politician, originally on the Bevanite Left, and a supporter of CND. He became party leader in 1983, apparently as part of Labour's swing to the left but he did much to defeat the militants and to make Labour more electable. He seemed likely to win the 1992 election but resigned the leadership after John Major's narrow victory.

John Smith (1938-1994) Scottish Labour politician who became Shadow Chancellor in 1989. He replaced Neil Kinnock as leader in 1992 and seemed likely to lead Labour to victory in the next election – but he died suddenly after a heart attack in 1994.

HOW FAR DID LABOUR RECOVER UNDER NEIL KINNOCK AND JOHN SMITH?

Although the real revival of Labour's fortunes is associated with Tony Blair and the emergence of New Labour from 1994, it is undeniable that Blair was continuing a process that had begun several years earlier. Even before the 1987 election, **Neil Kinnock** had taken a number of important steps, most famously his speech at the Bournemouth Party Conference in 1986 when he launched a direct assault on the militant tendency within the Party. Kinnock's attack was very effective because he had always had a strong position on Labour's Left, and because he was very good at party management.

The extent of Kinnock's success at bringing greater discipline to the Labour Party was obscured by Labour's third general election defeat in 1987 and the image of invincibility that now surrounded the Thatcher government. However, internal tensions within the Conservative Party were growing and Thatcher was beginning to lose a number of key members of her Cabinet, such as Parkinson and Whitelaw, and to fall out with others, such as Lawson, Howe and even previously loyal followers such as Norman Tebbit.

Meanwhile, the Labour Party machine at Walworth Road became increasingly effective and the emergence of **John Smith** as Shadow Chancellor gave Labour a capable, reassuring and more 'electable' face. It is sometimes forgotten amid the fascination with personalities that the main reason why Thatcher came under pressure from her own party by 1990 was that many Conservatives were convinced that they were likely to lose the next election if Thatcher remained. This reflected not only the slippage in Thatcher's position but also the marked revival in Labour's

Neil Kinnock.

John Smith.

Why was there such a dramatic Conservative decline and Labour recovery in the 1990s?   125

electoral credibility under Kinnock's leadership. As the 1992 election approached, many observers were anticipating a Labour victory.

Why did Labour lose the 1992 election?

The 1992 general election was widely expected to mark a turning point in British politics. The removal of Thatcher had taken away what many regarded as the Conservatives' trump card. The Conservative Party remained deeply divided over the 'regicide' of 1990 and John Major was an unknown quantity. The Kinnock–Smith team had achieved a remarkable degree of party unity and had also done much to modernise the party organisation. Many of the features associated with Labour's eventual victory in 1997 were already in place in 1992, such as the efficient polling and news management techniques of **Peter Mandelson** and other young modernisers. It was notable that political coverage in the national press, though still mostly pro-Conservative, was far less dismissive of Labour than before.

As the 1992 election campaign developed, the polls suggested a possible Labour victory. The race remained extremely close but in the closing stages of the campaign expectations of Labour success hardened into near certainty. Kinnock held an election rally at Sheffield that spilled over into something like a victory parade. This made the eventual outcome very bitter for Labour supporters. Ever since 1992, there has been a party mythology about the victory that was 'thrown away'. This mythology was based on several suppositions to explain how Labour had self-destructed, these were the premature triumphalism of the Sheffield rally, which had been counter-productive and lost the momentum of Labour's campaign, the tax-and-spend proposals of John Smith during the campaign, which had frightened key voters in 'Middle England' and Kinnock's personal failings as leader, especially his tendency to seem verbose and unfocused in his TV appearances.

This mythology, however, might seriously overrate the true situation: the 'certain victory' that was 'thrown away' may not have been so certain at all. There were many other possible reasons for John Major's surprise victory. Major himself proved a deceptively effective campaigner, especially when he started his series of 'soap-box' speeches. The Conservative Party chairperson, **Chris Patten**, coordinated the national campaign well. The tabloid press, especially *The Sun*, took a very forceful anti-Labour approach as the campaign ended and there was an unusually high proportion of undecided voters, so that opinion polls were more prone to error than usual. Moreover, the memory of the dark days of the 1980s was still uncomfortably close: perhaps Labour had not yet fully lived down its 'unelectable' image.

Peter Mandelson (1953-) Labour politician and grandson of Herbert Morrison, Mandelson was considered a master of the 'black arts' of political presentation and managing the media. He played a leading role in making Labour's election campaigns of 1992 and 1997 slick and disciplined.

Chris Patten (1944-) Conservative politician, often derided by Thatcherites as a 'wet'. As party chairman, he played a key role in John Major's election victory in 1992; but he lost his own seat at Bath and has never returned to Parliament. Major appointed him to be the Governor of Hong Kong, overseeing the handover to China.

HEINEMANN ADVANCED HISTORY

The tide turns for Labour

In retrospect, it is clear that the tide of politics was indeed flowing in Labour's direction in 1992 and the Party had come a long way from the depths of 1983. The Labour Party's 1997 electoral landslide under Tony Blair was based on many of the trends already in effect in 1992. Between 1992 and 1994, the new Labour leader, John Smith, was the focus of a steady rise in the popularity and political credibility of the Party.

Nevertheless, in 1992, the Labour recovery was not yet far enough for Labour fully to live down its recent history. There remained issues to be resolved and much internal party restructuring to be completed. Kinnock and Smith had laid the foundations of success but Labour would have to wait for several years of rebranding itself under new leadership (and several years of deepening internal Conservative divisions) before the long journey out of the political wilderness could be completed.

WHAT FACTORS LED TO THE DEVELOPMENT OF 'NEW LABOUR' IN THE 1990S?

Between 1992 and 1997, the political pendulum swung decisively towards Labour. Almost as soon as the election was past, Kinnock resigned the leadership and was replaced by John Smith. With his calm manner, likeable Scots accent and air of managerial competence, Smith was almost impossible to attack as a wild man of the Left. His Shadow Cabinet was full of bright rising politicians such as Gordon Brown and Tony Blair. At exactly the same time, John Major was beginning to discover just how difficult it would be to manage the Conservative government in the face of bitter internal feuds over Europe and a rush of political 'accidents', such as leaving the ERM, the BSE crisis and several Conservative MPs caught up in personal scandals.

John Smith was still in most respects 'Old Labour'. When he died suddenly of a heart attack in 1994, the process of modernising the Labour Party was still not complete. This process was to be carried through with spectacular consequences by the so-called 'Blair Project'.

There is another Labour myth about this. According to what might be termed the 'Blairite' view, New Labour represented a turning point in the history of British politics and of the Labour Party. The reasons given for this are as follows, it broke the outdated mould of Labour as the party of the trade unions and the working classes. It did for Labour in Britain **what the SPD in Germany had achieved** in 1959, and it did this above all by 'One Man One Vote' (which allowed the breakdown of block trade union voting at the party conference) and the abolition of Clause 4.

> ### KEY FACT
> **What the SPD in Germany had achieved** In 1959, the SPD (Socialist Party) in West Germany held a special conference to modernize its policies and to drop the commitments to Marxist ideas. After 1959, the SPD was accepted as a respectable, mainstream party. The Labour Party in Britain did not carry out this process until the 1990s.

In addition it ensured that Labour, not the Conservatives, became the party of discipline and unity, and of astonishing efficiency in modern public relations techniques. It enabled New Labour to escape from the grip of the 'Tory Press' and to gain support or at least acceptance from key national dailies like *The Sun* and it provided Labour with a dynamic and youthful leader capable of matching the wide appeal across the classes that Thatcher had enjoyed in the 1980s.

This myth can be challenged. For many commentators, the key issue in the 1990s was not the rebranding of New Labour but the implosion of the Conservative Party. Many left-wing MPs, such as Tony Benn or **Diane Abbott**, have continued to regard Blair as a maverick who does not represent the 'real' Labour Party. In his book *The Rivals* (2001), the BBC journalist James Naughtie analysed the tense relationship between Tony Blair and Gordon Brown as an unfinished struggle between the modernisers and more traditionalist Labourites for the soul of the party.

Once he had achieved his stunning victory in 1997 (and confirmed it with another thumping success in 2001), Tony Blair seemed to be both dominant and indispensable. For admirers and critics alike, Blair has often been seen as the natural successor to Margaret Thatcher. However, the past history both of the Labour movement itself and of the rapid and complete fall of the equally dominant and indispensable Margaret Thatcher gives pause for thought.

KEY PERSON

Diane Abbott
(1948-) Left-wing Labour MP speaking strongly on women's issues and on behalf of the Black community, especially in London.

1987	Margaret Thatcher's third general election victory.
1990	Riots against the poll tax; Margaret Thatcher replaced as Conservative Party leader by John Major.
1992	John Major's election victory with a small majority; John Smith elected Labour Party leader in succession to Neil Kinnock; 'Black Wednesday' and British withdrawal from the ERM.
1994	Tony Blair elected Labour Party leader after the death of John Smith.
1995	John Major challenged in leadership election.
1996	'Cash for questions' scandal.
1997	Referendum Party launched, splitting the anti-Europe vote; the decisive defeat of the Conservatives in the general election.

The decline of the **Conservatives and the revival of Labour fortunes, 1987–97.**

KEY PEOPLE

Alistair Campbell
(1957-) Tony Blair's press secretary. Along with Peter Mandelson, Campbell transformed Labour's image in the national press, especially the tabloids.

Neil Hamilton
(1949-) controversial Conservative politician accused of taking bribes to ask parliamentary questions. Hamilton was the best-known of several Conservative MPs who were involved in scandals over 'sleaze'. He lost his seat in 1997 to the journalist Martin Bell.

Norman Lamont
(1942-) managed John Major's campaign for the Conservative leadership in 1990 and Chancellor in 1992. Resigned in 1993 and became an outspoken opponent of Major.

WHY WERE THE CONSERVATIVES SO HEAVILY DEFEATED IN 1997?

The strengths of New Labour

The reasons why the Labour Party did much better in 1997 than in 1992, and the reasons why the Conservatives did so much worse, were numerous. The positive factors – the strengths of the Labour Party itself – were clear-cut. They included: Blair's leadership and image; the smooth running of the Party publicity machine under Peter Mandelson and **Alistair Campbell**; the discipline with which Labour candidates stayed 'on message'; perhaps, above all, the fact that New Labour was now finally distant enough from Labour's disastrous record during the 1980s. Although SDP politicians such as Roy Jenkins and Shirley Williams remained outside the Party, huge numbers of former Labour voters who had followed those politicians away from the Labour Party were now ready to vote Labour once again.

Conservative weakness and failure

The negative reasons – those concerning the weaknesses and failures of the Conservative government – make an equally convincing list. For many expert analysts, the core issue in 1997 was not a New Labour victory but an inevitable Conservative defeat. The Party was weakened, not only by divisions over Europe but by a rash of scandals culminating in the embarrassing downfall of **Neil Hamilton**, by doubts about John Major's leadership, and by staleness, after long years in power.

The BBC political editor John Cole once observed about the 1979 election, that the biggest force in elections was the conviction among voters that it was 'time for a change'. It may be that 1997 was just such a time and that Tony Blair did not achieve power through the brilliance of the 'Blair Project' but rather inherited victory from a tired and disintegrating Conservative government that had simply lost the appetite for power. Arguments for this view include the loss of the Conservatives' reputation for economic competence. On 'Black Wednesday' in 1992 John Major and his chancellor **Norman Lamont** were forced to pull Britain out of the ERM (Exchange Rate Mechanism) in a humiliating admission of economic failure. In 1998 Major told an ITV interviewer, 'that was the end. There was never any real hope after that!' Another argument looks at John Major's failure to cope with the problems of his leadership, and above all the internal rebellions of Eurosceptics. Major often seemed to be acting more as a Party whip than as a true leader – he even resorted to calling a leadership election within the Conservative Party in 1995, something no prime minister had ever been reduced to before. The 'desertion' of the Conservatives by national newspapers who had previously been natural supporters, often because of reservations over that same crippling issue of 'Europe', the continuing fall-out from 1990, which meant that bitterness over the 'betrayal' of Margaret Thatcher was never overcome (a problem made worse by the continuing high-profile contributions of the Iron Lady herself). In addition the impact of 'sleaze' and a rash of unrelated but damaging personal scandals such as **'Cash for questions'** which brought down Neil Hamilton. Labour was now widely seen as the Party of economic competence. In many ways, the Conservative Party never recovered from 'Black Wednesday' and the ERM crisis of 1992. And finally the social trends that were reflected in the average age of the membership of the Conservative Party – well above 60 years – and by the fact that New Labour fielded an unusually large number of youthful, often female candidates.

1997: a sea change in politics

In retrospect, the outcome of the 1997 election was a foregone conclusion. Nevertheless, just as in 1945, there were Labour supporters who hoped for victory but feared disappointment. For many observers, the sheer scale of the Labour majority was unexpected: the average swing to Labour across the nation was thirteen per cent. There had been a sea change in politics, symbolised by Labour victories in what had been very 'safe' seats such as Harrogate and Hove; perhaps the most striking feature was the defeat of so many high-profile Conservatives. Indeed, voters seemed to make an extra effort to ensure the rejection of Normal Lamont at Harrogate and **Michael Portillo** at Enfield.

The outcome of the 1997 election, therefore, in its sheer scale rather than in the mere fact of a Labour victory, created the impression of a turning point for Britain. The new intake of Labour MPs was younger, more inexperienced and more female than anything seen before. The rebranding of New Labour emphasised the sense of a break with the past. More than one observer compared the mood of 1997 with 1945.

KEY EVENT

'Cash for questions' scandal in 1994, two backbench Conservative MPs were accused of accepting bribes from lobbyists for asking questions in Parliament. Later, this scandal spread to include two ministers in the government, Neil Hamilton and Tim Smih.

KEY PERSON

Michael Portillo (1953-) originally on the Thatcherite wing of the party, he was defence secretary from 1985. He was one of the rebels against John Major after 1992, but did not stand in the leadership election in 1995. He sensationally lost his seat in Parliament in 1997, after which he began to re-invent himself as an inclusive moderniser.

CONCLUSION

In a manner similar to the general elections of 1951 and 1979, the 1997 general election clearly marked the end of an era: eighteen years of Conservative dominance came to an end. Thatcherism had apparently been decisively rejected and, for the first time in a peacetime election, Labour had won power with a strong majority.

The New Labour government was committed to a programme of radical constitutional reforms. In 1998, Tony Blair took a leading role in the negotiations culminating in the Good Friday Agreement (see pages 146–149), possibly ending 30 years of the 'Troubles' in Northern Ireland. In 2001, another decisive Labour election victory put Blair in line to be the first Labour prime minister ever to hold power for two full terms, perhaps even in a position to rival or surpass the record of success established by Margaret Thatcher.

Key questions

Several questions remain.

- Perhaps Thatcherism has not been rejected at all and Blair's government represents the continuation of Thatcher's legacy?
- Perhaps New Labour's new-found Party unity would not last – there might be a return to Old Labour ways and to in-fighting within the Party and the trade unions, even to a leadership split between Blair and Brown.
- Perhaps, now in government, Labour would suffer with its own divisions on the single currency.
- Perhaps the death of the Conservative Party has been exaggerated; perhaps the Tories will be reborn as a credible electoral force, just as Labour recovered from its near-death experience of the 1980s.

These questions are the stuff of contemporary journalism; the ultimate verdicts on the significance of 1997 will have to wait for a longer historical perspective. Nevertheless, it is possible to suggest that the period between the Second World War and 1997 makes a fascinating historical study. Within that 50-year time span, some patterns can be discerned allowing for lively differences of opinion.

It was the period of the Cold War. Was 1990–1 a happy conclusion, marking the victory of liberal capitalist democracies? Or did it mark the end of a period of unparalleled security, leading in the 1990s to an endless chain of small wars and the rise of global terrorism?

It was the era of the **Welfare State**. Was this a 'Golden Age' of social progress or an expensive drag on the free market economy?

It was the period of **economic recovery from the disasters of the Great Depression and the Second World War**. Was it a time of stable prosperity and ever-rising living standards? Or was it a time of continuous economic decline, of excessive trade union power and the 'nanny state', a time when Britain was overtaken by foreign competitors both from within and outside Europe?

It was the period of **European integration**. Was it a time when Britain gave up its dreams of empire and became a leading European partner within the European Community? Or a time when Britain was obsessed with the illusory 'special relationship' with the USA and repeatedly 'missed the European bus'?

It was the period of **social revolution**. Did Britain become a modern, multicultural society, or did it remain fundamentally traditional and nostalgic, a society still in the grip of the 'Establishment'?

It was the period of **two-party politics**. Was it an era of political continuity, with long spells of Conservative dominance briefly interrupted by interludes of moderate Labour governments? Or is it true to say that 1951, 1979 and 1997 were genuine political landmarks?

As usual, history offers no final answers; all historical judgements are provisional. All that students of history can do is to set out the alternative interpretations and perspectives, to analyse the evidence as best they can, to look their own prejudices in the eye, and then to make their own decisions.

A2 ASSESSMENT: BRITAIN, 1951–97

STRUCTURED SOURCE-BASED QUESTION IN THE STYLE OF AQA
Study topic:

The Miners' Strike of 1984 and the Conservative dominance of British politics under Margaret Thatcher.

Source A

In the 1983 election, Mrs Thatcher had General Galtieri's scalp on her belt; in 1987, she had Arthur Scargill's. The miners' strike of 1984 had turned into a virtual military operation. The police were, in effect, centralised and thousands of them were drafted from all over the country to confront the miners in their key northern pits. Civil liberties took a battering. The police set up roadblocks and, entirely at their discretion, forbade people from travelling. The strike itself was a mess. Scargill's manner made it almost certain that the NUM would lose. The miners in the key Midlands coalfields split away to form the UDM. Scargill also forced the strike at a time when the Coal Board, with government support, had built up huge coal reserves. Nevertheless, the strike was a closer-run thing than it looked and it divided the country. Even though it was the wrong strike at the wrong time, many people supported the miners and gave them money and food.

From *Miracle or Mirage?: The Thatcher Years* by P. Hirst (1997).

Source B

There were many faint hearts who believed that Mrs Thatcher had gone too far in her unflinching support for the police, who played a crucial role in preventing mass violence from triumphing. At times, during the course of the strike, defeat for the government seemed perilously close, but Scargill was never able to cut off the supply of coal to the main power stations, from the mines which continued to work, or from imports of coal transported from the docks by unionised drivers who did not support the NUM. Although the TUC and most of the unions gave support to the NUM, they were mostly reluctant to give much more than token help in case they ran foul of the law or had to face the hostility of their own members for backing an unpopular strike.

From *The Thatcher Effect*, edited by D. Kavanagh (1989).

Source C

The great coal strike finally ended in defeat for Arthur Scargill. It is a pity that the government made almost no political gains from one of the most important political events of my time in politics. For decades, governments had walked in fear of a coal strike. Now

Margaret Thatcher's government had broken not just a strike, but a spell. To make so little of it was poor thanks to the lorry drivers who risked their lives to carry coal, the steelworkers who rejected the miners' brotherly invitation to suicide-pact strikes, the dockers, or the police. Above all, it was poor thanks to those brave and decent miners who carried on working to save their jobs and their industry, and to save their country, too. I do not think anyone has properly assessed the skill with which the dispute was foreseen and then managed by the government. I doubt if any other prime minister would have had the courage to win a coal strike; yet, within weeks of that victory, we suffered heavy defeats in the local elections; the polls showed us in third place.

From *Upwardly Mobile*, the memoirs of Norman Tebbit (1988).

1(a) Use Sources A and C and your own knowledge.

How far do these sources agree in their explanation of the outcome of the miners' strike? [10 marks]

(b) Use Sources A, B and C and your own knowledge.

'The key to the Conservative dominance of British politics throughout the 1980s was the personality and decisive leadership of Mrs Thatcher.'

How justified is this claim? [20 marks]

Reading Before answering these questions, you should read A2, section 5. There is also an excellent brief analysis of Mrs Thatcher's approach to trade union opposition in *Hope and Glory: Britain 1900–1990* by Peter Clarke.

How to answer question (a) The key instruction here is to use your own knowledge as well as the evidence of the two sources. An answer solely based on the textual evidence of the sources will not score higher than level 2. A more effective answer would not only identify but also *explain* the degree of differences and similarities - using knowledge of the personality and political style of Norman Tebbit as a combative Thatcherite, supported by selective references to the tone and emphasis of the language he uses. Try to be concise and focus on the intentions and 'message' of each source, rather than a literal, descriptive approach to words and phrases.

How to answer question (b) This is a broader question, requiring a developed essay answer, in accordance with the marks allocated. The first essential task is to take sides; to set out a clear argued case that challenges or supports the key quotation. This case needs to be a balanced one – assessing the relative importance of Thatcher's 'decisive leadership' against other factors underpinning Conservative dominance (such as the fundamental weaknesses of the Labour Party at the time). It is also possible that you may wish to challenge the implicit pro-Thatcher assumptions in the quotation. It is vital, of course to make selective use of the sources but, first, you should set out your answer to the question and then use, not describe, how the source-evidence fits in with your case.

ESSAY QUESTION IN THE STYLE OF AQA
Study topic:

The decline of the Conservatives and the rise of the Labour party in the 1990s.

> Explain why the Conservatives were able to win the election of 1992 but were so heavily defeated in 1997. (20 marks)

Reading Before answering this question, you should read A2 section 6. There is also excellent, in-depth coverage of many aspects of this question in *Finest and Darkest Hours* by Kevin Jefferys.

Sample answer

When Margaret Thatcher stood down in 1990 as prime minister and leader of the Conservative Party after the leadership challenge from Michael Heseltine, it was John Major who won the subsequent leadership election and took power. For a time, he was even more popular than Thatcher had been at her peak, due to his 'normal' image and his conciliatory approach. Major was able to win a narrow victory in 1992 for these reasons and because he was continuing the popular policies of Thatcher but without her domineering style. Additionally, looming economic problems had not yet come to light at the time of the 1992 election.

After the 1992 election success, however, things rapidly started to go wrong for the Major administration. Dogged by 'sleaze', sex scandals and the 'cash for questions' affair, Major's government lost credibility and he earned a reputation for being dithering and indecisive; a reputation he was unable to shake off for the duration of his premiership, especially when splits over Europe widened. If Major had quickly disciplined the ministers concerned, his reputation would have been enhanced. But by neither disciplining them nor fully supporting them he came to be seen as a hesitant leader who could never commit himself. Major also suffered from being seen in the public eye as very boring, especially when compared to the energetic New Labour leader Tony Blair. Major's diminished reputation did play a role in the heavy defeat of the Conservatives in 1997, but this was outweighed by other political factors.

Margaret Thatcher's conviction politics had a profound effect on the Conservatives but also on politics in general (smashing the so-called post-war consensus) and especially on the Labour Party. After so long in opposition, it was clear that Labour would have to modernise. They were guided by the leadership of Kinnock, Smith and Blair in moving away from the hard Left and towards the middle ground of politics. They dropped Clause 4 and made themselves electable once again, promising to do the same things as the Conservatives, only more efficiently. This factor was of great importance in Labour's victory in 1997, much more so than Major's image problems. This was shown in the extent of Labour's relative recovery in 1987 and 1992 from the depths of the disaster of 1983.

Another significant factor in the 1997 Labour landslide was that the Conservatives had lost their reputation for economic competence. This occurred on Black Wednesday. When Britain entered the exchange rate mechanism, the then Tory government had overestimated the value of the pound and went in at too high a level. Huge amounts of money had to be spent on sustaining the value of the pound and more and more money was pumped in to try to do so. It became clear, however, that this could not continue and Britain crashed out of the ERM. This was a bad blow for the Conservatives as they had built their reputation on economic competence and this was now lost.

Other problems for Major included failures in areas such as his 'Back to Basics' campaign and the BSE crisis. But problems such as these merely contributed to the culmination of other more important factors in bringing about the fall of the Conservatives after eighteen years in power.

There were many reasons why the Conservatives lost so heavily in 1997, the most important of which were the modernisation of New Labour and the perceived loss of Tory economic competence after Black Wednesday. Other factors, such as the sleaze allegations, helped to ensure Conservative defeat and Labour's landslide victory.

Examiner's comments

This is a concise, selective answer which shows a particularly good grasp of synoptic issues. Conservative weaknesses are balanced against Labour strengths; the 1990s are seen in the context of the 1980s. There is also a careful attempt to differentiate between the relative importance of a range of factors. There might have been a little more direct attention to the actual campaigns in 1992 and 1997 and the conclusion is slightly disappointing since it merely repeats what has already been argued. Overall, however, this is a first-rate answer.

A2 SECTION: BRITAIN AND NORTHERN IRELAND, 1968–98

KEY TERMS

Unionists and Loyalists
moderate and hard-line Protestants.

Nationalists and Republicans
moderate and hard-line Catholics.

KEY EVENT

Battle of the Boyne, in 1690, Catholic rebels in Ireland were defeated by the forces of King William III (the Dutch prince William of Orange). This battle has been celebrated ever since by the Protestant community as a symbolic victory. The largest Protestant organization, the Orange Order, holds an annual procession headed by 'King Billy' on a white horse.

INTRODUCTION

The 'Troubles' in Northern Ireland lasted for almost exactly 30 years. They started with the civil rights campaign toppling into violence in 1968–9 and were brought to some sort of end with the Good Friday Agreement of April 1998. In between, more than 3000 people died. The 'Troubles' involved a clash of nationalisms, between **Unionists and Loyalists** on one side and **Nationalists and Republicans** on the other. However, the 'Troubles' were not confined to Northern Ireland and its people. They affected the London and Dublin governments and involved the USA.

Like the conflicts in the Balkans and the Middle East, the problems of Northern Ireland also involved past history. Few events happened without an immediate, usually disputed historical significance being claimed for them. Everything in the recent history of Northern Ireland is linked back to clashing interpretations of the **Battle of the Boyne** in 1690 or to the Irish rebellion of 1798 or to the Great Famine of 1845–51 or to the Easter Rebellion and Anglo-Irish conflict of 1916–21; or to Irish neutrality (often painted as sympathy with the Nazis) from 1939–45. After the onset of the 'Troubles', there was the never-ending 'politics of the last atrocity', with any Republican outrage always to be matched against the latest Loyalist action.

The linguistic minefield

In any interpretation of the 'Ulster Question', historians must also tread delicately through a linguistic minefield – the words one chooses to speak of the conflict are rarely neutral. The country itself has no universally accepted name: very different people would say 'Ulster' or Northern Ireland' as opposed to 'the 'North of Ireland' or 'the statelet in the north'. A city name can be a badge of identity: 'Derry' or 'Londonderry'? Labels are often loaded such as 'Orangemen', or 'Sinn Fein–IRA'?

There is hardly a historical event in which there cannot be detected a **Green** or **Orange** tinge. The most detached and would-be objective statement by a historian from outside the Province is likely to be furiously challenged within Northern Ireland, both by those claiming it to be a provocation to good Catholics and by those claiming it is the typical sell-out of all patriotic Protestants. Any A2 level student trying to assess the 'validity' of a historical judgement on recent Anglo-Irish history will therefore have to decide firmly what his or her own viewpoint is; sitting on the fence is just about impossible.

Understanding Northern Ireland also requires a 'cast of characters' – a clearly differentiated outline of the key personalities, parties and organisations involved in the politics of Northern Ireland. The following summary is far from comprehensive (and is doubtless highly controversial!); it should be seen in the context of changes over time.

Green Green is historically the colour of Irish nationalism. Tim Pat Coogan's book on Irishmen outside Ireland, for example is titled *Wherever the Green is worn* (1998).

Orange
Orange is the colour of Unionist Protestantism. The largest Protestant organisation, The Orange Order, takes its name from William of Orange, the Dutch prince who became King William III in 1688 and was victorious at the Battle of the Boyne.

Republicans	**Loyalists**
'Official IRA'	Ulster Volunteer Force (UVF)
Irish National Liberation Army;	Loyalist Volunteer Force (LVF)
'Real IRA'; Continuity IRA	Billy Wright, Johnny 'Mad Dog'
Provisional IRA	Adair
Provisional Sinn Fein	Ulster Defence Association (UDA)
Gerry Adams	Progressive Unionist Party (PUP)
Martin McGuinness	(David Ervine)
Nationalists	**Unionists**
SDLP	Ulster Unionist Party
John Hume	David Trimble
Gerry Fitt	Democratic Unionist Party
Alliance Party	Ian Paisley
	The Orange Order
The Irish dimension	**The British dimension**
The Church in Ireland	The Northern Ireland Office
Fianna Fail	Labour Party
Garret Fitzgerald	Conservative and Unionist Party
Fine Gael	The British army
Albert Reynolds	
Bertie Ahern	
Americans	
'NORAID'	Bill Clinton
Irish–Americans	George Mitchell

The sheer intensity of rival partisan perspectives makes the relatively short period of 30 years crowded and complicated. The following timescale may provide a useful basic framework.

KEY PERSON

Ian Paisley
(1926–) has been
a leading hardliner
since the 1960s,
opposed to any
concessions to
Nationalists. He
set up the DUP
(Democratic
Unionist Party) in
1971 as a direct
challenge to the
official Unionists.

1921–68	The 'Stormont Ascendancy'
1968–9	The origins of the 'Troubles'
1969–74	The bloody stalemate
1980–6	The hunger strikes and the rise of Sinn Fein
1993–8	The 'peace process'

History, of course, never ends. The Good Friday Agreement may ultimately peter out inconclusively; large-scale violence may yet return to the streets. **Ian Paisley** and his supporters may yet turn a majority of Unionists against the Agreement. Nevertheless, should that happen, it that will belong to another episode. The story of the 'Troubles' between 1968 and 1998 has already become History. Reaching conclusions about that History presents a challenge; what follows is a tentative guide to help students on their way.

WHAT WAS THE RELATIONSHIP BETWEEN BRITAIN AND IRELAND BEFORE THE 'TROUBLES'?

For those born since the late 1960s, with their memories of the never-ending 'Troubles' and the ever-present television images of marches, paramilitaries and bombings, it is difficult to realise how little mainland Britain was aware of Northern Ireland before 1968. There was a vague knowledge of Unionism as an element associated with the Conservative Party. There was an awareness of sectarian hatreds, often in connection with the football loyalties of Liverpool and more especially Glasgow. Some older people had memories, often bitter ones, of the Irish Republic having remained neutral or, in some eyes at least, 'pro-Hitler' during the Second World War. There were parts of the country with significant Irish communities and with strong links to Ireland either North or South. For the most part, there was little knowledge or interest.

Partly, this was because within Northern Ireland, the situation was essentially static. The IRA was weak; politics and society were stuck in the groove of the so-called 'Stormont Ascendancy'. At Stormont, the Belfast Parliament, a monolithic Unionist majority controlled Ulster politics. The Unionists were part of the Conservative Party and occasionally vital to ensuring its majority at Westminster. The prime ministers of Northern Ireland could rely on an automatic political control. Protestant organisations such as the Orange Order could rely on permanent influence over the political and economic life of the Province. The Nationalist Catholic minority lived in clearly demarcated districts and felt themselves to be trapped in a position of economic inferiority and political helplessness. The prospects of social and political change were slight, not least because the dominant Protestant majority did not want change.

Factors for change

However, by 1968, change was indeed likely to occur. Northern Ireland was to be influenced by significant social and political trends from the world outside. The 1960s was the decade of 'social revolution' and student protest; this was to have powerful effects on the Sixties generation in Northern Ireland, above all in the symbolic 'year of youth' in 1968. The 1960s was also the decade of civil rights in the USA; notably enhanced by the power of television, the Civil Rights Movement was to provide a model for radical Nationalists. It was the decade of the Left, of Che Guevara and the rise of the ideologies and techniques of urban terrorism; this strongly influenced a new generation of the IRA. And finally the 1960s was a time when the so-called 'Welfare State generation' grew up; there was the emergence of an educated Catholic middle class, less ready to accept the status quo.

By 1968, these forces for change were pushing upwards. The old certainties of the Stormont Ascendancy were about to be blown away.

WHY DID THE 'TROUBLES' BEGIN IN 1969?
The Civil Rights Movement

The key pressure for change in 1968 came from the Civil Rights Movement. Opinion in Britain, mostly very indifferent to Northern Irish affairs, was quite easily persuaded, once it did become aware of the issues, by arguments in favour of equality of opportunity. The original leaders of the Civil Rights Movement were a long way from terrorists. They made reasonable demands. Moreover, the Civil Rights Movement, at first, was not purely Catholic and claimed to be non-sectarian. The Labour government in London, led by Harold Wilson, had more sympathy with civil rights and reform than with Protestant Unionism.

In late 1968 and early 1969, the Civil Rights Movement was met by Loyalist violence and overtaken by counter-violence and the rise of the Provisional IRA. Why this happened is relatively easy to explain in terms of events and personalities; but it is impossibly difficult to reach any accepted conclusions as to who was to blame.

The Civil Rights Movement launched an effective campaign of marches and protests in 1968. At this time, the IRA was both weak and divided, and the onset of violence in 1969 caught the IRA unprepared. Its leader, **Cathal Goulding**, was regarded as obsessed with left-wing ideology. As the violence spread, so those IRA men who took a more traditional approach to the use of force gained more support. This was how the Provisional IRA came into existence, on the streets in 1969, even though the movement as it is known today did not formally emerge until January 1970.

KEY PERSON

Cathal Goulding (1922-1998) Marxist theorist who was leader of the 'Official' IRA in the late 1960s. Impatience with his intellectual approach helped lead to the formation of the Provisional IRA.

Terence O'Neill
(1914-1990) the
Unionist Prime
Minister of
Northern Ireland
from 1963. In
1968, O'Neill
offered a package
of reforms to
meet the demands
of the civil rights
movement but he
could not control
the polarization of
politics and
resigned in 1969.

**James
Chichester-
Clark** (1923-)
Unionist Prime
Minister of
Northern Ireland
after Terence
O'Neill.
Although he
reluctantly
abolished the B-
Specials, he failed
to prevent the
widening political
violence and was
replaced by Brian
Faulkner in 1971.

It is easy to set out the chronology of the origins of the 'Troubles', but interpretation of these events is obviously controversial. Was it a case of nationalist grievances being manipulated by Republican extremists, or a violent 'Protestant backlash'? Was it simply a misjudgement of the situation by the British government and army commanders? At the end of this chapter there is an assessment exercise based on a range of sources about this controversy.

1968	October: Violent incidents during the civil rights march in Derry. December: Televised speech by **Terence O'Neill**, promising reforms.
1969	January: People's Democracy march from Belfast to Derry attacked at Burntollet Bridge. February: Failure of O'Neill to gain sufficient support in Stormont elections. April: Resignation of O'Neill; replaced by **James Chichester-Clark**. August: Londonderry Apprentice Boys march stoned by Catholics; attacks on the Catholic 'Bogside' by 'B' Specials; violent rioting in Belfast against Catholic districts; British troops sent to Belfast and Derry. October: Disbandment of the 'B' Specials recommended by the Hunt Report; Protestant attacks on the British army – first army fatality.
1970	January: Split between the Official IRA and the new Provisional IRA; coordinated violence against RUC and British soldiers. June: Formation of the moderate nationalist SDLP; the Wilson government defeated and replaced by Edward Heath; violent rioting in Belfast; the British army now focused on repression of the Republican threat.

The origins of the 'Troubles', 1968–70.

WHY DID BRITAIN FAIL TO ACHIEVE A SOLUTION IN THE 1970S?

British governments, both Labour and Conservative, were slow to realise the full extent of the challenges they faced in Ireland from 1969–70. It took time for a coherent policy to be developed, either in security matters or in dealing with the Irish governments in Dublin. For much of the time the governments in London reacted to events as they happened. Realisation was also slow to dawn on Loyalists and Republicans. Loyalists continued to wish for something they simply could not have – a return to the pre-1969 status quo of the 'Stormont Ascendancy'. Republican extremists like **Sean MacStiofain**, flushed with the apparent successes of the **Provos**, had a naïve belief that it really was possible to 'bomb the British out of Ireland'.

The most emotive event of these early years was the killing of fourteen civilians when the British army fired on a protest march in Derry in January 1972; this polarised opinion and gave a spectacular propaganda victory to the IRA. However, the decisive event of 1972 was the end of Stormont. The last Northern Ireland prime minister, **Brian Faulkner**, clashed with the Heath government over security policy and resigned. This led to the introduction of Direct Rule from Westminster. This was the end of the old 'Stormont Ascendancy' and the beginning of the long search for an alternative system, which meant some form of power sharing between Nationalist and Unionist communities.

Although the Heath government came close to success in 1974 with the Sunningdale Agreement, which was a power-sharing government for all political parties in Northern Ireland. It was only in the 1990s that a meaningful peace started to become a realistic possibility. The Good Friday Agreement was very similar in its essence to what had been rejected in 1974. It may be that success was achieved in 1997 where it had not been in 1974 because parties on all sides had discarded their illusions and learned at last to accept reality.

The complex events of 1970–4 included a number of dramatic 'turning points', notably the launch and failure of **internment** in 1971, '**Bloody Sunday**' in 1972, and the collapse of the Sunningdale Agreement in 1974. As usual, there have been conflicting interpretations of the failure to find a solution, of which the following forms only a small selection:.

- 'If only the army and the security forces had been given a free hand.'
- 'If only Heath had not called a general election at such a sensitive time.'
- 'If only the Wilson government had been willing to face down Loyalist blackmail in 1974.'

It may be, however, that no solution was possible at that time because the essential partnership between the London and Irish governments did not yet exist and because the extremists on both sides still held illusions that it was possible to achieve outright victory. From 1974, the 'Troubles'

KEY PERSON

Sean MacStiofain (1928-) was chief of staff of the Provisional IRA in the early 1970s, committed to a policy of 'all-out war' against the British Army.

KEY TERM

Provos the nickname of the Provisional IRA.

KEY EVENT

Internment interning terrorist suspects without trial had been used successfully in the 1960s; but in 1971 the policy failed. It was seen as one-sided, and was based on poor intelligence. Innocent citizens were arrested and many of the main targets escaped.

KEY PERSON

Brian Faulkner (1921-1977) Unionist prime minister of Northern Ireland in 1971 and 1972. Faulkner persuaded Heath's government to introduce internment in 1971.

1970	July: British Amy curfew imposed on Catholic Lower Falls area of Belfast.
1971	Resignation of Chichester-Clark; replaced by Brian Faulkner. August: Internment without trial of Republican suspects. December: Total deaths reach 174; 15,000 British troops stationed in Ulster.
1972	January: Thirteen civilian deaths on 'Bloody Sunday' in Derry. February: British Embassy in Dublin burned down by Republican protesters. March: Meetings between Provisional IRA and the opposition leader, Harold Wilson; the end of Stormont – the resignation of Faulkner and the start of Direct Rule. July: 'Operation Motorman' – British army action against 'no-go' areas.
1973	December: Meeting of Unionists, **SDLP** and Alliance parties with Heath at Sunningdale in Berkshire.
1974	January: Power-sharing Executive established by the Sunningdale Agreement. February: Westminster general election during the miners' strike; many successes for anti-Sunningdale Unionists. May: Loyalist Workers' Strike organised by Unionist politicians and the **UDA**; collapse of the Power-sharing Executive and a return to Direct Rule.

The search for a solution, 1970–4.

continued in an established pattern of sectarian violence and conflict between the army and Republican paramilitaries, including a growing tendency to carry the 'armed struggle' to the mainland, as with the **Birmingham bombings of** 1974.

It is significant, that the war between the Republican paramilitaries and the security forces and the authorities never completely excluded compromise and negotiations. Provisional IRA representatives had negotiated with Harold Wilson as opposition leader in 1972 and as prime minister in 1974. Such secret negotiations continued to occur on and off. British governments constantly claimed that they would 'never speak to terrorists' but this was never really true. The successful negotiations in the 1990s were not a new development but the continuation of a trend that had begun twenty years before.

HOW SERIOUSLY WAS THE NORTHERN IRELAND ISSUE AFFECTED BY THE HUNGER STRIKES IN 1980–1?

Between 1974 and 1985, the situation in Northern Ireland was a bloody stalemate, dominated by the 'politics of the last atrocity'. There was little sign of any political movement. Then, in 1980 and 1981, the political map was altered by the dramatic impact of IRA hunger strikers and the sharp rise in electoral support for Provisional **Sinn Fein**.

The hunger strikes grew out of IRA protests against being treated as criminals rather than as political ('special category') prisoners. These protests began in 1976 in the H–Block prison as the dirty protest by IRA men 'on the blanket'. This campaign grew into a major confrontation with the new government of Margaret Thatcher. Although the first hunger strikes in 1980 caused little stir, the renewed hunger strikes in 1981, especially the death of **Bobby Sands**, had a major impact. The Thatcher government faced down the strikes and, publicly, 'won'; but the government soon afterwards made big concessions to the prisoners' demands and the hunger strikes were widely seen as a success, especially in winning support for Sinn Fein in other countries, above all the USA.

The biggest impact of the hunger strikes was on Republican politics. At first, Sinn Fein had opposed the hunger strikes. After their success and the huge crowds following Bobby Sands' coffin, the new younger leadership of Sinn Fein made the decision to contest parliamentary elections. There was also a shift in the leadership of Sinn Fein to Northern Catholics led by **Gerry Adams**. In 1983, Provisional Sinn Fein did spectacularly well in elections both locally and in the general election. By 1986, the new strategy of fighting on two fronts with 'the Armalite in one hand and the ballot box in the other' was well established.

Protestors in support of those on hunger strike, April 1981.

KEY EVENT

Birmingham bombings, 1974 in 1974, the IRA bombed two pubs in Birmingham known to be used by British troops off duty. Many were killed and injured. This was the first time the 'Troubles' had spread to England; it led to the 1975 Prevention of Terrorism Act.

KEY TERM

Sinn Fein Like the IRA, the name Sinn Fein went far back into Irish history but the significant fact in 1980-81 was the emergence of 'Provisional Sinn Fein' as the political wing of the Provisional IRA.

KEY PERSON

Bobby Sands (1954-1981) Sands became famous as the first of the hunger strikers of 1981 to die.

Gerry Adams
(1948-)
Republican
activist and
president of the
PSF. MP for West
Belfast from 1983
to 1992 but
refused to take his
seat at
Westminster. His
talks with John
Hume paved the
way for the IRA
ceasefire of 1994
and for the 'peace
process'.

Garret Fitzgerald
(1926-) Leader
of the Fine Gael
party in the Irish
Republic in the
1980s. He became
Taioseach (Prime
Minister) in 1983.
In 1985 he
negotiated the
Anglo-Irish
Agreement with
Mrs Thatcher.

John Hume
(1937-) a civil
rights activist in
the 1960s, Hume
succeeded Gerry
Fitt as leader of
the SDLP in
1979. His
attempts to bring
Sinn Fein into the
political process
culminated in his
talks with Gerry
Adams in 1994
and the IRA
ceasefires.

The Anglo–Irish Agreement, 1985

The Thatcher government had a hard-line image but was forced into cooperation with Dublin by the rise of Sinn Fein. Between 1982 and 1985, complex negotiations led to the Anglo–Irish Agreement, signed at Hillsborough Castle in 1985. Several factors made this easier for Thatcher these included the role of **Garret Fitzgerald**, a moderate Taoiseach elected in 1982, the report of the New Ireland Forum, founded by **John Hume** in 1983, and pressure on Thatcher from the USA by President Reagan.

The Anglo–Irish Agreement was furiously opposed by Unionists, both by Reverend Ian Paisley's hard-line Democratic Unionist Party (DUP) and by the mainstream Ulster Unionist Party (UUP). In 1986, by-elections were held, forced through by the resignations in protest of Unionist MPs; there was widespread violence against the RUC Royal Ulster Constabulary (the police service of Northern Ireland) and the army by Loyalists. Like Sunningdale in 1974, the Hillsborough Agreement was blocked by a Unionist backlash. Nevertheless, it was a major step forward in links between London and Dublin.

1979	Victory of Margaret Thatcher in Westminster general election; murder of her close friend Airey Neave during the election campaign.
1980	Collapse of first hunger strikes by IRA prisoners demanding 'special category' status.
1981	March: New wave of hunger strikes led by Bobby Sands. October: Hunger strikes called off by strikers' families after ten deaths; decision by Provisional Sinn Fein to contest elections.
1983	May: 35 per cent of popular vote won by Provisional Sinn Fein in local elections. June: Gerry Adams elected as Westminster MP for West Belfast. November: Gerry Adams elected President of Provisional Sinn Fein.
1985	November: Anglo–Irish Agreement signed by Thatcher and Garret Fitzgerald.
1986	January: By-elections after mass resignation of Unionist MPs. March: Violent campaign against RUC by Loyalist paramilitaries.

Hunger strikers and the rise of Sinn Fein, 1979–86.

WHY WERE MOVES TOWARDS PEACE POSSIBLE IN THE 1990S?

Between 1986 and 1993, Northern Ireland seemed once again frozen in its permanent cycle of violence and counter-violence. These were the years of the killing of an IRA cell in Gibraltar, of the Remembrance Day bombing in Enniskillen, the 1991 IRA mortar attack on 10 Downing Street, and countless other acts of terrorism by both sides. This violence continued until 1992, when the third, successful phase of the search for a peaceful solution began.

This phase was not as sudden as it seemed. Much of the peace process between 1992 and 1998 was based on the foundations of previous failed initiatives. However, the key factors were two unlikely partnerships. The first was between John Hume and Gerry Adams. In theory, this should not have been possible – Provisional IRA and the SDLP were political rivals (the IRA had made frequent attempts to assassinate the previous SDLP leader, **Gerry Fitt**). Nevertheless, from 1988 onwards, Hume persisted in trying to win Adams over to a peaceful strategy: over months during 1992 and 1993, he succeeded. The 1993 Hume–Adams document was the very rough basis of the final settlement in 1998.

The second partnership was equally unlikely – between John Major and **Albert Reynolds**. Major and the Conservatives were always more sympathetic than Labour politicians to the Unionist side; Reynolds came from the Fianna Fail party, with a long record of suspicion towards the British and especially the Conservatives. The successful later partnership between Tony Blair and **Bertie Ahern** was much easier to understand. However, Major and Reynolds made vital beginnings, precisely because they were able to take with them the natural opponents of cooperation. (Their relationship was constructive but it was not all sweetness and light. After one stormy private meeting, an aide asked Reynolds how things had gone. 'He chewed the bollocks off me,' said the Taoiseach, 'but I took a few lumps out of him').

After the general election of 1992, these two partnerships worked in parallel, leading to the Downing Street Declaration of 1993, the 1994 paramilitary ceasefires and to the close involvement of President Clinton and his skilful, patient envoy George Mitchell. The election of Tony Blair in 1997 accelerated the final steps to negotiation and agreement.

This process was always on a tightrope and there were dangerous interruptions by stalled negotiations and acts of violence. However, the key question behind all other questions was whether, this time, there would be an agreement that was not brought down by a Loyalist backlash. Predictably, Ian Paisley and the DUP were flatly opposed; but

Gerry Fitt (1926-2002) Catholic nationalist politician, and leader of the SDLP until 1979. He was a bitter opponent of the IRA who made several attempts to murder him.

Albert Reynolds (1932-) became leader of the Fianna Fail party after Charles Haughey. Although regarded as a traditional, anti-British republican, he established a good relationship with John Major, leading to the Downing Street Declaration.

Bertie Ahern (1951-) leader of Fianna Fail after Albert Reynolds. His partnership with Tony Blair and his good relationship with President Clinton did much to bring about the success of negotiations leading to the Good Friday Agreement.

KEY PEOPLE

James Molyneaux
(1920-)
traditionalist
leader of the
Ulster Unionist
Party prior to
David Trimble.
Took part in the
early negotiations
with John Major's
government in
1993 and 1994.

Mo Mowlam
(1949-) was
appointed
Northern Ireland
Secretary by Tony
Blair in 1997.
Mowlam did
much to keep the
paramilitaries
involved in the
peace process. Her
unorthodox, hard-
swearing style
offended unionists
and traditionalists
she was replaced
by Peter
Mandelson in
1998.

David Trimble
(1944-) leader of
the UUP from
1994. Originally
seen as a hard-
liner, he took the
leading role on
the Unionist side
in negotiating the
Good Friday
Agreement.

1992	April: Sinn Fein loses to the SDLP in the Westminster general election.
1993	September: Joint statement agreed by John Hume and Gerry Adams. December: Downing Street Declaration by John Major and Albert Reynolds.
1994	January: Visa from President Clinton allowing Gerry Adams to visit the USA. March: Three-day Provisional IRA ceasefire. August: 'Complete cessation' of IRA campaign of violence. October: Ceasefire declared by Loyalist paramilitaries. December: George Mitchell appointed as President Clinton's mediator.
1995	August: **James Molyneaux** replaced with David Trimble as leader of the UUP. November: Visit to Belfast by Bill Clinton.
1996	February: IRA ceasefire ended with Canary Wharf bombing.
1997	May: Landslide election victory of Tony Blair. July: New IRA ceasefire. October: Beginning of negotiations at Stormont, chaired by George Mitchell.
1998	January: **Mo Mowlam**'s visit to Maze prison to win over Loyalist paramilitaries. April: Good Friday Agreement signed by all parties. June: Elections to the new Northern Ireland Assembly.

The road to the Good Friday Agreement, 1992–8.

the UUP leader **David Trimble**, elected as a presumed hardliner in 1995, was able to carry the Agreement through. The Loyalist paramilitaries were persuaded, only just, to stick to the 1994 ceasefire although the IRA broke one down in 1996 only to be redeclared in 1997.

Why was the 1998 agreement successful?

Why success was achieved in April 1998 where it had never been possible before is a complex question with many different answers. Relations between Tony Blair and the Taoiseach Bertie Ahern were the best that the London–Dublin relationship had been. The US influence, through

President Clinton and George Mitchell, was more persuasive than ever before, especially in raising hopes for the economic benefits of peace. John Hume's endless optimism made a huge difference. However, the biggest single factor may have been the changed mentality of the paramilitaries.

Eamon Collins was an IRA gunman who changed his mind. In 1995, he went public, through a TV documentary and a book, *Killing Rage*, in which he gave vivid descriptions of paramilitary violence. Shortly afterwards, as he knew in advance would probably happen, he was murdered as an act of Republican revenge. Here are some of the reasons he gave for turning away from IRA violence, when he described meeting a notorious Loyalist hard man, Gusty Spence:

For an instant, I could only see before me a deadly enemy of my people. I was filled with a killing rage, all the old anger coming back. But the feeling passed and my rage subsided. I knew that murder was the logical result of that rage, and murder would not solve anything. At that moment, I realised how far I had travelled in my life.

Collins did not represent all the gunmen; after all, he was killed for writing his book. Many Loyalists objected to the 1994 ceasefire; dissident IRA men carried out an awful bombing in **Omagh** after the Good Friday Agreement had been signed. Nevertheless, there were enough Republicans, such as Collins, ready for an end to the unwinnable war. On the other side were people such as **David Ervine**, who converted from terrorism to become the spokesperson for the PUP and a key voice in favour of peace and reason. This mixture of war-weariness and realism among the paramilitary organisations was perhaps the missing link that allowed peace to win in 1998.

The road to the Good Friday Agreement was long, slow and strewn with dangerous obstacles. The first IRA ceasefire broke down and was only reinstalled in 1997 after another bombing campaign. The annual march to Drumcree Church at Portadown caused massive controversies, especially in 1995. Throughout there were difficult pressures on the Unionists who felt that more and more concessions were being forced out of them. David Trimble was vital to the peace process reaching a successful conclusion.

Who deserves credit for the Good Friday Agreement?

The all-important question about 1998 is why it happened – why was it achievable then but not before? In apportioning credit for this success, it is possible to see many contributions on many levels. The mediation of Senator George Mitchell (and, behind Mitchell, the commitment and

KEY EVENT

Omagh bombing after the Good Friday Agreement was ratified in a referendum, there was a backlash from dissident republicans claiming that Sinn Fein had 'sold out'. In August 1998, a group called 'Continuity IRA' set off a huge car bomb in the market town of Omagh. 29 civilians were killed. Revulsion against the atrocity probably strengthened support for the Agreement.

KEY PERSON

David Ervine (1954-) was another case of terrorist seeing the light. He gave up violence and became the leading political spokesman for the PUP (Progressive Unionist Party) the political wing of the LVF.

persistence of the Clinton Presidency): it can be argued that no successful negotiations would have been possible without the patience and skill and, above all, the neutrality of Mitchell's chair. Also the partnership between Tony Blair and Bertie Ahern: all previous attempts to solve the Northern Ireland problem had been undermined by divisions between London and Dublin. (Although the original breakthrough had been made in 1993 and 1994 by the unlikely partnership between John Major and Albert Reynolds.) The persistent efforts of John Hume and the SDLP in persuading Gerry Adams to join the peace process were also important. Hume and David Trimble won the Nobel Peace Prize for their efforts; it is ironic that one key result of his success was to vastly increase the voting support for Sinn Fein at the expense of his own SDLP. The realisation by the Provisional IRA leadership that the war to 'bomb the British out of Ireland' could never be won. The mirror image of this point is the claim that, by the early 1990s, the security forces had decisively 'defeated' terrorism. Also the cynical decision of paramilitaries on both sides to play along with peace negotiations in order to secure the release of prisoners. And finally, the all-important of David Trimble in persuading the bulk of Northern Ireland Unionists to accept the Agreement. This success owed much to Blair and Mitchell in convincing Nationalists and Republicans that Trimble and the Unionists had to be given support and encouragement.

CONCLUSION

The Good Friday Agreement of 1998 marks the dividing line between history and current affairs. What happened in 1998 was the end of a defined period of the 'Troubles' since 1969. Whether the Agreement takes permanent root or not, the history of Northern Ireland was fundamentally changed by it.

This short chapter cannot begin to explain all the complex issues of the 'Troubles'. Many important events and individuals have been left out; many questions and debates have been left unresolved. The key to understanding Northern Ireland is not to know all its bewildering events in detail; rather, it is a matter of perspectives. The A2 level student needs above all to develop his or her own interpretation of the 'Troubles'. There are no 'right' answers, only your own judgements – then it will be possible to evaluate critically the many partisan perspectives on the 'Ulster Question': Loyalist and Republican, Nationalist and Unionist, British, Irish, American, socialist, liberal, conservative, politician, historian or journalist. This is, of course, a challenge – but also a source of fascination.

At the end of this section, there is a sample examination question on the

A2 ASSESSMENT: BRITAIN AND Northern IRELAND, 1968–98

STRUCTURED SOURCE-BASED QUESTION IN THE STYLE OF AQA
Study topic:

The origins of the 'Troubles' in Northern Ireland 1968–1969.

Source A

4000 people took part in the civil rights march in August 1968. It was the first time in the Six Counties that the civil rights song *We Shall Overcome* was heard. The route was from Coalisland to Dungannon, where it was to conclude with a rally in the market place. Police prevented this rally because of what became a familiar tactic – the Paisleyites had organised a counter-demonstration. Even so, the march passed off peacefully, unlike the repeat march in Derry in October. It should be explained that it was not the idea of marching for civil rights that was new – it was the idea of Catholics marching. Marching in the Six Counties was something the Orangemen did as of right and the Catholics did on sufferance.

Adapted from *The Troubles* by Tim Pat Coogan (1996).

Source B

On 5 October 1968, a peaceful protest march at Londonderry was baton-charged by the RUC. Northern Ireland's reformist leader, Captain Terence O'Neill, met with the British premier Harold Wilson. On 22 November, to the disgust of his own 'ultras', O'Neill announced a reform package going a long way to meeting Catholic demands. After more marches and a violent response by Protestant ultras trying to stop peaceful protests, O'Neill made an emotional televised appeal to all sections of the community. He asked: 'What kind of Ulster do you want? A happy and respected province or a place torn by riots, regarded by the rest of Britain as a political outcast?' The appeal struck a chord with the moderate majority, including the leaders of the Civil Rights Movement, who called a truce over Christmas. But Bernadette Devlin and others in the student-led People's Democracy Movement had another agenda. Devlin described O'Neill's broadcast as 'hilarious', adding: 'the students called no truce'.

Adapted from *The Irish War* by Tony Geraghty (2000).

Source C

In the first few days of 1969, the pause in violence and confrontation was broken by the deliberately provocative 'People's Democracy' march from Belfast to Londonderry. Young people, many of them students, were cynically used as bait to attract the expected and hoped-for Loyalist attack, which could then be exploited to arouse community antagonisms. In the aftermath of this march, there was serious rioting in Londonderry for several days, putting the RUC under impossible pressure and resulting in breaches of discipline that further alienated the Catholic community.

Adapted from *Memoirs of a Statesman* by Brian Faulkner (1978).

1a   Use Source C and your own knowledge.

How valid is the interpretation offered by Faulkner in Source C of the slide from peaceful civil rights protest towards violence in 1968–9?   [10 marks]

b   Use Source A and your own knowledge.

How reliable is Source A as evidence about the impact of civil rights marches in the autumn of 1968?   [10 marks]

c   Use Sources A, B and C and your own knowledge.

'The renewed IRA campaign was not what the idealistic majority of civil rights campaigners thought they were in business for; their peaceful revolution was high-jacked before it had even got started.'

How justified is this view of the origins of the 'Troubles' in 1968–9?

[20 marks]

Reading Before answering these questions, you should read the A2 section on Britain and Ireland. It is also essential to be familiar with the five nominated texts listed in the AQA specification. In addition, there is an excellent and up to date account of these events in Chapters 2 and 3 of *Making Sense of the Troubles* by David McKittrick and David McVea.

How to answer question 1(a) Before assessing Brian Faulkner's interpretation, it is essential to have a clear grasp of what your *own* interpretation is. Faulkner's views are pro-unionist (and perhaps with an element of self-justification). How far do you consider these views to be justified in the context of your understanding of the issues? Are there other interpretations that you feel are more 'correct'?

How to answer question (b) The reliability of any source depends on how well it is informed; how far its intentions may be partisan or prejudiced; and on the extent to which it is corroborated by your own knowledge of the events. In this case, Coogan has to be judged as an exceptionally experienced and well-informed journalist, but also as a man with strongly pro-republican views. It is up to you to make an overall assessment and to use selected specific evidence from the source in support.

How to answer question (c) This question requires a developed essay answer, in accordance with the marks allocated. Note that the actual question, about the origins of the Troubles in 1968-69, is wider than the quotation, which is about how the civil rights campaign, slid over into violence. First, you should be ready to set out your own argument explaining the onset of the Troubles and then analyse the quotation to explain how far it is justified, or not, and how it fits into the broader question. Selected material from the three sources should, of course, be included in your supporting evidence; the best answers will also refer to wider reading from the nominated texts and beyond.

BIBLIOGRAPHY

WORKS PARTICULARLY RELEVANT TO AS STUDENTS

POLITICS AND SOCIETY IN BRITAIN, 1929–64

P. Adelman, *The Rise of the Labour Party, 1880–1945* (Longman, 1996)

D. Aldcroft, *The Interwar Economy: Britain, 1919–39* (Batsford, 1970)

G. Best, *Churchill: A Study in Greatness* (Penguin, 2002)

J. Black, *Modern British History since 1900* (Macmillan, 2000)

A. Calder, *The People's War* (Jonathan Cape, 1969)

P. Catterall (ed.), *Britain, 1918–51* (Heinemann, 1994)

T. Downing and J. Issacs, *Cold War* (Bantam, 1998)

K. Jefferys, *The Attlee Governments, 1945–51* (Longman, 1992)

A. Mayer, *Women in Britain, 1900–2000* (Hodder & Stoughton, 2002)

R. Pearce, *Contemporary Britain, 1914–79* (Longman, 1996)

R. Pearce, *Attlee's Labour Governments, 1945–51* (Routledge, 1994)

M. Roberts, *Britain, 1858–1964: The Challenge of Change* (Oxford University Press, 2001)

J. Stevenson and C. Cook, *Britain in the Depression: Society and Politics, 1929–39* (Longman, 1994)

WORKS PARTICULARLY RELEVANT TO A2 STUDENTS

CHAMBERLAIN AND APPEASEMENT

P.M.H. Bell, *The Origins of the Second World War in Europe,* 2nd edition (Longman, 1997)

J. Charmley, *Chamberlain and the Lost Peace* (Papermac, 1989)

R. Cockett, *Twilight of Truth: Chamberlain, Appeasement and the Manupulation of the Press* (Weidenfeld & Nicolson, 1989)

M. Gilbert, *The Roots of Appeasement* (Weidenfeld & Nicolson, 1966)

R.A.C. Parker, *Chamberlain and Appeasement* (Macmillan, 1993)

A.J.P. Taylor, *The Origins of the Second World War* (Penguin, 1962)

D.C. Watt, *How War Came: The Immediate Origins of the Second World War, 1938–9* (Heinemann, 1989)

POLITICS AND SOCIETY IN BRITAIN, 1951–97

C. Barnett, *The Lost Victory* (Papermac, 1995)

P. Clarke, *Hope and Glory: Britain, 1900–90* (Penguin, 1996)

C. Cook and J. Stevenson, *The Longman Companion to Britain since 1945* (Longman, 1999)

E. Heath, *The Course of My Life* (Hodder & Stoughton, 1999)

P. Hennessy, *Prime Minister: The Office and its Holders since 1945* (Penguin, 2000)

E. Hobsbawm, *Age of Extremes: The Short Twentieth Century, 1914–91* (Abacus, 1994)

W. Hutton, *The State We're In* (Jonathan Cape, 2000)

P. Johnson (ed.), *Twentieth Century Britain: Economic, Social and Cultural Change* (Longman, 1994)

A. Marwick, *The Sixties* (Oxford University Press, 1998)

B. Maddox, *Maggie* (Hodder & Stoughton, 2003)

A. Mayer, *Women in Britain, 1900–2000* (Hodder & Stoughton, 2002)

K.O. Morgan, *The People's Peace: British History, 1945–90* (Oxford University Press, 1992)

B. Pimlott, *Wilson* (HarperCollins, 1992)

A. Seldon, *Major: A Political Life* (Phoenix, 1997)

A. Sked and C. Cook, *Post-war Britain: A Political History, 1945–92* (Penguin, 1993)

N. Tiratsoo (ed.), *From Blitz To Blair* (Phoenix, 1998)

H. Young, *One of Us: A Biography of Margaret Thatcher* (Macmillan, 1989)

BRITAIN AND NORTHERN IRELAND, 1968–98

L. Clarke & K. Johnston, *Martin McGuinness: From Guns to Government* (Mainstream, 2001)

E. Collins, *Killing Rage* (Granta, 1998)

T.P. Coogan, *The Troubles: Ireland's Ordeal, 1966–96* (Arrow, 1996)

R. English, *Armed Struggle: The History of the IRA* (Macmillan, 2003)

T. Geraghty, *The Irish War: The Military History of a Domestic Conflict* (HarperCollins, 2000)

E. Mallie and D. McKittrick, *Endgame in Ireland* (Hodder & Stoughton, 2001)

H. McDonald, *Trimble* (Bloomsbury, 2001)

D. McKittrick and D. McVea, *Making Sense of the Troubles* (Penguin, 2001)

George Mitchell, *Making Peace: The Making of the Good Friday Agreement* (Heinemann, 1999)

P. Routledge, *John Hume* (Pimlico, 1999)

The five titles nominated as required reading for Unit 6WU in the AQA History specification are:

Tim Pat Coogan, *The IRA* (HarperCollins, 2000)

S. Wichert, *Northern Ireland Since 1945* (Longman, 1999)

C. Kennedy-Pipe, *The Origins Of The Present Troubles In Northern Ireland* (Longman, 1997)

J. Loughlin, *The Ulster Question Since 1945* (Macmillan, 1998)

T.G. Fraser, *Ireland In Conflict, 1922-1998* (Routledge, 2000)

INDEX